DIGITAL INSIGHTS 2020

MICHAEL DE KARE-SILVER

DIGITAL INSIGHTS 2020

HOW THE DIGITAL TECHNOLOGY REVOLUTION IS CHANGING BUSINESS AND ALL OUR LIVES

Matador
9 Priory Business Park
Kibworth Beauchamp
Leicestershire LE8 0RX, UK
Tel: (+44) 116 279 2299
Fax: (+44) 116 279 2277
Email: books@troubador.co.uk
Web: www.troubador.co.uk/matador

ISBN 978 1783064 731

British Library Cataloguing in Publication Data.
A catalogue record for this book is available from the British Library.

Typeset in 11pt Aldine401 BT Roman by Troubador Publishing Ltd, Leicester, UK

Matador is an imprint of Troubador Publishing Ltd

Contents

The digital world in 2020

1. The Technology Revolution   1

2. A few big companies already dominate   7

3. Imagine the World in 2020   9

Blueprint /case studies /lessons for managing digital transformation

4. Digital Transformation: key lessons and success factors   21

5. Digital Transformation: "how-to" blueprint   29

Impact on HR, skills, people

6. What is the HR impact of digital on future talent needs and hiring   38

7. 5 keys to finding the best digital talent   44

8. How the workplace will change and the workforce will need to adapt   49

The Digital Organisation: building the most effective team and structures

9. Omni vs Multi-channel: the new organisation paradigm   60

10. The 3 Pillars for organisation design   65

11. Building a successful e-commerce business:
    how to establish the "virtuous cycle"of sustainable
    self-funding growth and development   71

12. Case study: e-Commerce team structure for ABC Company   76

13. Impact of Digital on Marketing /Marketing Department
     organisation structures   85

14. Multi-national Marketing:
     impact of digital on organisation structures   90

e-Commerce /e-Business

15. Retail time bomb!   95

16. e-Commerce international expansion in Europe:
     the immediate potential   98

17. B2B Social Media   107

18. How should B2B companies be taking advantage of "Digital"   110

Making it happen!

19. Digital check-list for making it happen!   118

20. Case studies: building a successful online business-lessons learned   125

Chapter I

The age of the Technology revolution

There is a truly disruptive but exhilarating revolution taking place. Technology has moved into a new era. Digital is changing the way we communicate, the way we buy things, the way businesses interact, the way we talk. Our expectations of what we can do and how we can do it have been transformed. The "i-want-it-now", time poor, technically literate developed world now demands the convenience of being able to do things "my way". I want the anytime, anyhow, anywhere world. I rely on it. It governs my life

There's a complete transformation taking place. Technically we've moved at an incredibly rapid pace in past 30 years. We could say we're now in the seventh stage of recent evolution:

Main frame
▼
Mini computers
▼
Desktop
▼
Internet
▼
Mobile
▼
Cloud/ Social
▼
Open Source / ecosystems

The pace of these developments, as also observed in a recent Morgan Stanley report, has accelerated. If mainframes took some 20 years to reach mass commercialisation, mobile has taken about 7 and social has taken about 3. Whether you talk Moore's Law or more simply the billions of dollars of private equity investment, there is a huge amount of continuing R&D and an absolute wealth of ideas and pipeline of new products that are all queuing and lining-up to find their own commercial life-changing, business breakthrough applications.

Where is all this heading? What are we likely to see as this decade unfolds? Can we even begin to imagine our world in 2020? Who could have predicted the current scene 10 years ago? Who would have imagined that traditional business models would be so much under threat? Who could have predicted a Facebook or the dominance of Apple and Google? Who could have foreseen that online commerce would have destroyed bricks 'n mortar book shops, record shops, video hire, changed for ever the way we buy travel, insurance, the way we bank, buy clothes and electricals, our ability to search the world for bargains, the ease with which a business in London can find customers in China (and more typically the other way around!). A century ago we saw the demise of old cotton mills and the collapse of manufacturing in the West as we gained access to lower wage costs and lower prices in Asia. We look back at some of these historic changes and ask: why didn't the big companies of the day move with the times? Why did great businesses become dinosaurs? And we wonder what great corporations of now will become the dinosaurs of tomorrow? Will companies like Microsoft for example continue to have such a vice like grip on computer operating systems? If the trend to mobile internet access and mobile computing continue, then might the current dominating OS from Apple and Google Android supplant that Seattle monolith?

Just twenty years ago the only computers that were in use were in corporations and even then most people did not have one on their desktop. Now they are everywhere and the way we interact with them has fundamentally changed. Human beings think they are in control. But are we? We have become completely dependent on digital machines and equipment. We rely on them completely. Without them we are lost. If we lose our mobile we are distraught. In one recent survey, the one thing people said that they would be most upset about losing, was their mobile. It ranked higher than the credit card, jewellery, your car and even your pet dog or cat! "it is my most treasured possession".

And we are all expecting computing use, access and application to continue to develop and improve. We can now access 24/7 from most anywhere. It used to be a world of point and click, now we touch and it's like simply pressing a button. Already many talk to their computer and voice command and voice recognition software is improving all the time. How much longer before the computer talks to us? Such technology already exists. The computer (can be programmed) to switch itself on at say 6.30am, give us our wake up call and offer a cheery good morning in whatever tone of voice we have selected. As we're getting showered and dressed it can be telling us about our schedule for the day. We can say "book taxi" and (through a simple pre-programme) and computer Q&A confirm location and time. We can voice emails and text messages. We can even send through a repeat shopping order. We can tell our computer to schedule a delivery next time we're home, book a restaurant, arrange our travel, do anything which can be reduced down to automated digital communications. How soon before this sort of interaction and expectation becomes the norm? In fact have computers already taken control? Here are a few recent headlines:

- "Algorithms take control of Wall Street" (Wired.com)
- "Computer drives car without human control" (Science Daily)
- "Computers to replace teachers" (Daily Telegraph)
- "Technology is taking over the planet" (Helium.com)
- "Computer hardware and software will match the human brain by 2020" (US Robotics Institute)
- "Thinking/learning machines may not be that far away" (NYT/ IBM report)

In the novel "Nine Tomorrows" Isaac Asimov portrays a futuristic world where computers do control humans. Asimov describes how humans become dependent. No need to read books or study. Why bother when the computer already has that knowledge and you can access it when you want? Just rely on computers! Computers start to select from their vast store of knowledge what to teach humans. They make their own priorities and start shaping what humans know. They start to keep some knowledge away from humans and just for their own data banks, for themselves. Computers start to control humans' lives.

Far-fetched? While Asimov is critical of this future dependency, we are already close to it. Google's algorithms decide what we see and in what order we see it. Medical diagnostic software tells physicians what the problem is and what treatment is required. Traffic control systems automatically regulate air traffic and auto routes. Our old-fashioned "Point and Click" world, where we controlled what we would look at is quickly morphing into a two-way "Touch and Talk". It won't be long before we expect the computer to start learning about us. Recognise our voice, anticipate our regular commands. As we stop needing to stare at a screen then our desire for continued "screen-less", interactive, intelligent communication can take us into a Stephen Spielberg / Tom Cruise "Minority Report" type world where what 10 years ago was pure science fiction now becomes a reality.

Who will be the companies that are the providers of these applications and solutions? Who are the new kids on the block? What seems to be happening is that in our new world, smaller more agile companies have the best chance to succeed. They can access the funds, (at least if they're on the US West Coast they can… try getting true *venture* capital in Europe!), they can leverage remote but global partnerships, they can interact and share work-in-progress easily and cost effectively. Tech start-ups will be all the rage. Here are just a few examples of top 100 tech companies from Innovation.com:

– **Anboto** provides technological solutions to enable an easy and smart interaction in natural language between customers and computers
– **Natural User Interface Technologies (NUITEQ)** is a Swedish multi-touch software technology company, which facilitates people to engage with touch screens using multiple fingers simultaneously.
– **Canatu Oy's** business is the production of a new class of versatile carbon-based components based on carbon nanotubes. These components improve the performance and reduce the cost of optical energy generation and storage and electrical devices while simultaneously reducing their environmental footprint.
– Semaphore from **Smart Logic i**s an innovative tool in taxonomy management and automatic knowledge classification. It builds the connections between topics, entities and resources. This semantic intelligence enables users to quickly manage, find, explore and use content
– **ID-U** offers a new concept in biometric identification. It is the first stimuli-driven biometric system. The technology is based on the uniqueness of a person's eye-movement patterns. Utilization of a user's kinetic response to construct his identification signature is called 4D-Biometrics.

Alongside the on-going march of technology innovation, there are a number of big transformation themes that are going to shape this decade:

(i) The rise of the MCE, the Multi-Channel Enterprise

(ii) The demise of the retailer traditional bricks 'n mortar model

(iii) The development of major new online distributors and intermediaries for products and services, replacing the Tescos and Wal-Marts of the old world

(iv) Human computer interaction will change from "point and click" to a world of "think talk move"

(v) The shift from "push" advertising and marketing to "pull" user generated buzz.

(vi) The need for major "business model reengineering and transformation" to survive this new world

(vii) Automation breakthroughs will see more and more everyday tasks done by machines

(viii) Cost structures in the Cloud will enable more radical and global low cost solutions

(ix) The "great divide" between those with digital access and those without

(x) The need for the workforce to reskill

2020 is not that far away. The pace of change is such that what's in the lab today can quickly become the killer app of tomorrow. The iPhone and iPad show just what can happen if a company can get the user interface right. Apple hit the magic button with those new products. They have shown, very clearly, what it takes to succeed. And the answer is simple: you need the software breakthrough plus, and it's a big plus, you need to make it fascinating and amazing to interact with it. A great example is the Gesture Cube (see later) where interactive 3D steps out of the movie and becomes real!

All corporations are now at a cross-roads. They can either examine their future or embrace the new digital world. Or they can keep their head down and hope that its real impact will be delayed. For many their future "strategy" is still only looking out at most 12 months. The excuse is: how can we look out any further when the world is changing so rapidly. This short-termism allows execs to develop an incremental holding path where a mix of cost cutting and fighting to maintain customer contracts might just about deliver some kind of acceptable budget plan. And after all, there's always the old credit crunch to blame and its dampening effect on consumer spending and business investment.

But eventually this type of "strategy" is just not going to work. Eventually the new players and rivals will reach critical mass with their new software and approaches. Eventually consumer behaviour will change to such a degree that for example a big retailer just will not need all that space to merchandise and display products when it's all available more conveniently online. That may happen in 3 years or 5 but the impact of this technology revolution will be felt, it will not go away or lessen. And so that cross-roads is here. And companies need to decide what to do about it.

Chapter 2

A few big companies already dominate!

It's clear that our future world of communications and business is being radically changed by digital technology and innovation. What's startling is that this is being master-minded by just a few multi-national organizations. They already are dominating and their influence is going to grow.

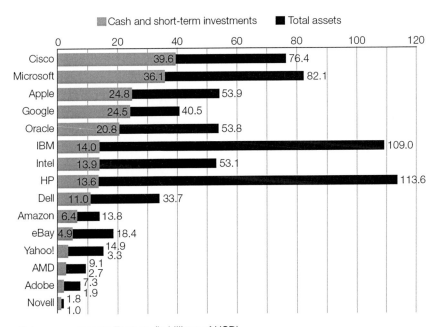

Data source: Google Finance (in billions of USD)

Google own YouTube. They also own DoubleClick, AdMob and a host of other general and niche market-leading businesses. They have acquired more than 100 companies. They have invested in fields as diverse as robotics, gesture and facial recognition and wind turbines! They vigorously promote Google Chrome web browser as an alternative to Internet Explorer, Google Cloud, Android (the now global leading mobile phone operating system), Earth and Maps, Google

TV, Google Glass and many other truly innovative applications. And they have spent $12.5bn acquiring Motorola to provide more global access.

Microsoft has spent $4bn snapping up Nokia, buys Yammer (the leading enterprise social media network) for $1.2bn cash and $8.5bn of its cash reserves acquiring Skype, a substantial premium given Skype was at best break-even and certainly not making a profit. But it does give Microsoft access to a 663 million global community. It has a 1.6% share of Facebook and a small shareholding (albeit <5%) in Apple. It has acquired some 150 other companies or strategic stakes in the past 20 years.

Google, Microsoft and a few other dominant global tech companies together have huge cash war chests. Microsoft had some $35bn at time of writing, Apple had c. $25bn and Google had some $25bn. And other Tech companies like IBM, Cisco, Intel, HP and Amazon are all cash rich. In fact, the top 12 Tech companies listed in the US have a staggering $215bn of cash searching for investment opportunities. They are among the most valued on the planet.

These are the companies that are changing our lives. These are the ones that are leading the biggest revolution in history. These are the ones that are set to continue to lead the transformation of the global economy and the way human beings interact and communicate. Even as we read this book, history is being made.

Chapter 3:

Imagine the World in 2020

Today our digital world is largely based on "Point and Click". It's what we do. We're still largely chained to our desk with our PC. We move a cursor across the screen and click. Web sites are built that way and e-commerce is driven that way. User journeys are written that way and web analysis and metrics are managed that way. We're contained within a small rectangular box with a standard screen resolution of fixed pixel-array display of typically1024 x 768 (though we also now see 1440 x 900 as screens get bigger). We live with tool bars across the top and often bottom of the screen taking up to 25% of the space. That's how web pages are designed. It's how we think about the computer and it governs the principal way we use digital technology and how we interact.

But inevitably and inexorably we are starting to move away from this constraining form of interface and interaction. And the breakthrough really has been touch technology. Invented as far back as 1971 by a Dr Sam Hurst while at the University of Kentucky, it then took a number of years to move out of the lab and into the real commercial world. Citibank became the pioneers. In 1986, they ripped out their old button and keypad ATMs in New York and Hong Kong and replaced them with a simple touch screen user interface. That move had the same market place impact then as the iPhone has had more recently. It was revolutionary and innovative and changed the way enterprising businesses thought about new product development. Not long after, we started seeing touch screen kiosks in-store. The first nationwide interactive kiosks were found in the Florsheim shoe store chain across the US. They were basic and at that time lacked any internet connectivity but were product information focussed and because they were new and at that time had a novelty value they attracted plenty of interest. Apple themselves were already very active in exploring this area and they launched the forerunner of the iPhone/iPad in 1993 with their Apple Newton.(An alternative but similar device at the time was the Palm Pilot and these two devices between them dominated the then handheld market sector).

Source: Apple

The Apple Newton was not intended to be a computer but a "personal digital assistant" or PDA (a term coined by Apple's then CEO John Sculley who was really the key creator of Apple). It used touch screen and stylus pen enabling users to manage information such as Notes, Calendar, Contacts, Schedules etc. The built-in handwriting recognition was one of the major new features and attracted a lot of interest developing ideas about subsequent computer interaction which need not only be driven by mouse and keyboard. But the Newton and Pilot were bulky at over an inch thick, heavy, weighing at about one pound and of course at that time in mid 1990's had no wireless internet capability, though they could be connected via cable to the PC to at least sync up data.

And all these developments were preparing the ground for the iPhone, iPod, iTouch and iPad which have now made touch screen technology widely available, exciting to use and moving quickly to become a default user interface.

So we're starting to move away from a world of "Point and Click". We're arriving at the next stage on the journey. It's now about simple "Touch and Go!"

The "old", desk-based and wired computer environment we've grown up with is starting to look distinctly dinosaur-like! It's as though computing has been in a dark and primitive phase. Our desks have been covered with cables. We've been surrounded by boxes and routers and modems. We've been living in a spaghetti junction. If we've wanted to take advantage of digital technology we've had to become experts in configuring ports, formatting drives, understanding our server SMTP spec, wrestling with ISPs, worrying about RAM capacity, negotiating data caps on broadband subscriptions… the logistics of operating and interacting in the digital world have been complex, can deter many and certainly slow down rates of uptake and adoption.

So the iPad has been so well received because it starts us on the road to where all these roadblocks are a thing of the past. Here's a potentially dream machine that can combine all the major computing and communication functions in one convergent device. It's portable. It's wireless. It's glossy and sleek and feels good. It's very responsive and intuitive. It connects with us directly and intimately. It works and will mark an historical shift in computing and digital interaction.

Source: Apple

But this is just the start of the next phase and era of computing and human interaction.

It's only a matter of time before Speech Recognition software reaches a level of reliability and accuracy that it will become more widely incorporated in our everyday computer interaction. Although the first "speech recogniser" was developed in 1964 and exhibited by IBM, it took another 30 years of lab work before it was ready to be considered for a full commercial roll-out. Microsoft were unsung pioneers here and they developed their own speech recognition technology which was first made widely available in Office 2003. It has since evolved so it is embedded in all Microsoft Windows and Office products. Apple Macs have been slower to adopt this functionality but they now have their own award-winning product called Dictate

What does this Microsoft and Apple software do? There are two core functions. The first is Dictate, turning speech into text. The second is Command. Speak and the computer will respond. The Microsoft and Apple software tools have their rivals. Dedicated speech recognition software providers like e-Speaking, TalkingDesktop and TalktoyourComputer all offer a variety of features such as voice commands already built-in and ready to activate eg Open Email, File Open, Select, Next Page etc. Such is the competition that these software tools are available on free trials and download with low subsequent one-off license or monthly payments. There are also specialist tools eg for the medical/health care profession so that more arcane vocabulary is more easily and quickly recognised.

The claim is for around 90% accuracy today and improvements on that as the computer gets used to your voice. Of course it's a further step from point and click. What's more, the computer is now also being given its own voice to speak back. For the present that is restricted to response like "File is Opened", "Job is Complete". But this "computer response ability" is very much at an early stage of development and is not yet at an interactive level. The next stage is Computer Prompt. This is a function where the computer will talk to you: "New Email" is an obvious one, but that is evolving to calendar/meeting alerts: you're next meeting is in 30 minutes. And as devices converge we could expect to hear eg: you have a call waiting from your partner, shall I put you through? Or hurry up, you're late for your next meeting! Is this just a few steps away now from the computer Hal in the avant-garde Kubrick movie 2001 where Hal is in fact able to act independently? And while that is a stimulating idea, such an invention is without doubt outside (sadly?) the 2020 timeframe of this book (even the most gung-ho futurologists I have spoken to agree that genuine artificial intelligence is beyond this decade)

However, why is the voice recognition trend critical? Just as the iPad has innovated around touch and has tapped into that very intimate set of tactile and intuitive response mechanisms. So devices are being developed that can truly integrate and harness the ability of speech as well. It means that we can now start to enter a digital world which is much closer to" Touch and Talk."

It's exciting because it is now much more about the computer being "wired" into our brain, rather than into the router. It taps much more into a wider range of our core senses. All of a sudden instead of it all just being about what you can see, the whole experience becomes much more immersive and engaging. We are connecting with much more of our core being. It's now about Sight and Sound and Touch and Talk. Our bodily senses are being connected, not just our brains. And that's why devices that can exploit this are so successful. Only Smell and Taste remain completely elusive, for the time-being...

So we are moving away from Point and Click. We are firmly into an era of "Touch and Go!". Only a matter of time before further voice integration takes us into "Touch and Talk". But is that the end of the journey?

Not surprisingly, the answer is that over this next decade till 2020 there is already the next evolution ready and waiting in the wings. Early prototypes are out of the lab and are available to buy. They may still be a bit clunky but they are the next stage of our future and the next step in digital technology development.

Gesture Cube is the latest innovation that points the way to yet a further stage of progress. It uses electric field sensing technology to make 3D spatial hand or finger movement tracking possible. It also employs proximity detection technology. It provides a 3D interactive experience. It detects your hand's approach and movement and responds to your gestures. You just wave your hand to control the device! These natural hand movements interact with a computing device to become the means of navigation, image and content movement and selection. The hand gestures are intuitive and effortless and can indeed feel magical.

Gest-Cube 3D technology is currently being featured on a new product from Indent Technology (based in Germany) working in partnership with design engineers Lunar, who are based in Palo Alto.

This product is currently being marketed as a home entertainment device. Wave your hand, navigate and choose. Select what music you want to listen to, what photos or videos to share and in what order, what movies to watch. But the technology itself works outside of this Gesture Cube product. It could for example enable 3D hand control on 2D screens so it could work on a smart phone or tablet PCs, picture frames and iPads.

Another initiative in this arena which is recent but already widespread is the

X-Box Kinect. This does use different technology but looks to achieve a similar end result allowing remote unconnected hand movement to control what takes place on screen. Kinect relies on range camera technology developed by the Israeli company Prime Sense. This in effect determines 3D scene information from a continuously projected infra-red structured light. The Kinect camera and software provide full body 3D motion capture as well as facial and voice recognition capabilities. Kinect can track up to two active players for motion analysis and can track 20 joint movements at any one time.

Kinect is similar to Gesture Cube in some ways in that it is utilising software to track remote movement and the camera technology gives an extended practical range of about 3 metres. And while of course current developments at Xbox are focussed on Gaming and new game experiences, Kinect has also served a purpose in bringing hand controlled remote wireless 3D interaction into the mass market and moving consumer expectations and acceptance along another notch.

It means we're getting ever closer to a world which was first showcased in the Tom Cruise film *Minority Report*. This was a Stephen Spielberg directed movie which came out in 2002. Spielberg wanted to present a plausible future world and is said to have consulted with a number of scientists and technologists to provide a more realistic and authentic future scenario. 15 experts convened at a now famous 3 day "think tank" session. These included architect Peter Calthorpe, Douglas Coupland, computer scientist Neil Gershenfeld, biomedical researcher Shaun Jones, computer scientist Jaron Lanier, and former Massachusetts Institute of Technology (MIT) architecture dean William J. Mitchell. So there was some real in-depth thought and input that was being captured.

What was so innovative and exciting about this movie and why did its "sci-fi realism" strike such a chord? It was simply because you could sense that technology was in reach. Even though the technology did not exist in reality in 2002, nevertheless people could see how likely it could be and could believe in this future world. What is extraordinary is that 10 years later a lot of the ideas in the movie are now in fact fast becoming real.

The most powerful visual idea in the movie was the way in which Cruise interacted with computer-generated imagery. He was able to tell the computer to bring up a 3D holographic display of various screen pages and images from a computer memory bank. He could interact with that imagery using voice commands or by touch. Like with an iPad today he could stretch, shift, zoom, extend, move to the "next page" with simple touch or what could become a

Gest-Cube like hand wave. It was as though he was interacting seamlessly and completely with 3D and holographic displays. There was no sense of there even being pages from a computer, it was just content and material which could be summoned, moved and sorted. The way Cruise's manipulation of content and imagery was presented in the film was as if he were conducting an orchestra. But this was an orchestra of content, not just people. They called it the "spatial operating environment interface".

Source: Imdb.com and Ign.com

News and information sources from Wikipedia and elsewhere have noted the future technologies depicted in the film were prescient. The Guardian published a piece titled "Why *Minority Report* was spot on". And the following month Fast Company examined seven crime fighting technologies in the film similar to ones now actually becoming available. National Radio published a podcast which also analyzed the film's accuracy in predicting future technologies. One of the big ideas in the film was said by Hewlett-Packard to have been a major motivator to conduct further research – in HP's case to develop cloud computing.

Technologies from the film later realized include:

- Multi-touch interfaces put out by Obscura, MIT, Intel, and Microsoft for their Xbox. A company representative, at the premiere of the Microsoft Surface, promised it "will feel like Minority Report". When Microsoft released the Kinect motion sensing camera add-on for their Xbox gaming console, the Kinect's technology allowed several programmers, including students at MIT, to create what they called "*Minority Report* inspired user interfaces".

- Retina scanners, by a Manhattan company named Global Rainmakers Incorporated (GRI). The company is installing hundreds of the scanners in Bank of America locations and has a contract to install them on several United States Air Force bases.

- Insect robots, similar to the film's spider robots, developed by the US Military. These insects will be capable of reconnoiter missions in dangerous areas not fit for soldiers, such as "occupied houses". They serve the same purpose in the film – according to the developer, BAE Systems, the "goal is to develop technologies that will give our soldiers another set of eyes and ears for use in urban environments and complex terrain; places where they cannot go or where it would be too dangerous."

- Facial recognition advertising billboards, being developed by the Japanese company NEC. These billboards will theoretically be able to recognize passers-by via facial recognition, call them by name, and deliver customer specific advertisements. Thus far the billboards can recognize age and gender, and deliver demographically appropriate adverts, but cannot discern individuals. According to *The Daily Telegraph*, the billboards will "behave like those in… *Minority Report*… in which Cruise's character is confronted with digital signs that call out his name as he walks through a futuristic shopping mall. IBM is developing similar billboards which plan to deliver customized adverts to individuals who carry identity tags. Like NEC, the company feels they will not be obtrusive as their billboards will only advertise products which a customer is interested in. Advertisers are keen to embrace these type of billboards as they figure to reduce costs by lowering the number of adverts wasted on uninterested consumers.

- Electronic paper, developments announced by Xerox, MIT, media conglomerate Hearst Corporation, and LG the electronics manufacturer. Xerox has been trying to develop something similar to e-paper since before the film was released. In 2005, when the Washington Post asked the chief executive of MIT's spin-off handling their research when "the "*Minority Report*" newspaper" would be released, he predicted "around 2015. Tech Watch's article, '*Minority Report*' e-newspaper on the way", noted that Hearst was "pushing large amounts of cash into" the technology. In discussing the LG announcement, Cnet commented that "if you thought electronic newspapers were the stuff of science fiction, you're quite right. They first featured in the film *Minority Report*, released in 2002!"

So all this starts to bring colour and life to our future world and one that is very much just around the corner. In less than 10 years much of Spielberg's vision is fast becoming reality. The old dinosaur days of "point and click" will soon become a distant memory. We are moving through Touch and Go! through to "Touch and Talk" and are beginning to see signs of a Cruise type/Gest-Cube/3D interactive type world that can be described as "Command and Connect".

As if this is not enough, we also have developments around "brain-driven" computer control where implants in the brain can be used to order and control the computer screen.

We are at the early stages of controlling computers just by thinking. Thought control has had especial early application for people who are paralysed. An article in Nature magazine shows how someone paralysed from the neck down can nevertheless control a computer, play games, change channels on TV, and manipulate a robot just by thinking: "Think and Move!" This brain to machine connection is getting ever closer and has relied principally on implanting electrodes to respond to the electrical activity associated with certain movements. An alternative method being trialled places electrodes on the scalp and the computer learns to associate particular brain signals with intended actions. A recent CeBIT show saw the launch of the world's first patient-ready commercially available brain computer interface. And there are many companies experimenting with such devices. And the cap that sits on the scalp to capture the brain movement is becoming more user-friendly and easier to wear. It's assumed that eventually no cap will be needed and the computer will be controllable just by thoughts alone. In the same way that a computer can recognise voice, it can also be "taught", it's believed, to remotely scan and pick up the brain's electrical impulses. (The picture here is of the Emotiv wearable headset which starts to make useable what was once functional and ugly)

Source: Emotiv EPOC neuroheadset

In fact, according to latest announcements from Intel, "chips in the brain will control computers by 2020". Researchers at Intel have concluded that it will only be a matter of time before we see the end of the keyboard and the mouse and surf the Net using just our brain waves. The brain would be enhanced by Intel-developed sensors that are implanted. Experiments are currently taking place with robots and there are already examples of manipulating a robot using the brain of a monkey! It may sound far-fetched but the Intel research and 2020 deadline is serious. And this leads us on inevitably and inexorably to one of the ultimate medium term goals of developing genuine artificial intelligence. There are today many research teams across the globe looking at how to integrate software to enhance the processing speed and power of the human brain and to potentially add new knowledge immediately via a plug 'n play routine!

Significant effort is currently being devoted to making human interaction with computers and with information in general more simple, natural and seamless. "The pace of advances in computing, communication, mobile, robotic and interactive technologies is accelerating dramatically", Ahmed Noor points out in a recent review in Mechanical Engineering. "The trend towards digital convergence of these technologies with information technology, virtual worlds, knowledge-based engineering and artificial intelligence is beginning to usher in a new era"

And Noor goes on to say: "there will be a dynamic aggregation in the future of humans, cognitive robots, virtual world (cloud-based 2.0) platforms and other digital components to create a new ecosystem. Humans will have multi-sensory, immersive 3-D experience and capability in a mixed physical and virtual world… the emphasis will be on optimising human performance"

The human experience of the computer to date has been for us to immerse ourselves in it, we have had to learn to work in the computer's world of scroll bars, list controls, mice and key board. But we don't live there. Even with the iPhone we are still interacting with the device on its terms in its world. But, we exist in our own three dimensional world. And what will start to happen is that the computer will increasingly come to us. It will start to recognise who is sitting in front of it or who is holding it. It will recognise our voice and react when we talk to it. Breakthroughs such as the Xbox Kinect and Gest-Cube show that the computer can learn to react to *our* physical movements and the advance in BCI (brain computer interaction) demonstrate further how we will be able to exert control, on our terms and in ways that suit us, not chained to the desktop!

Here's one vision of the future from Sam Martin speaking at a Forbes magazine conference about our world in 2020:

Source: Media@frogdesign

"In the future every visible thing will be catalogued and indexed, ready to be instantly identifiable and described to us. Want to go shopping? In the future we won't need big retail stores with aisles of objects on display. We'll be able to shop out in the virtual world. Do you like that new car you saw drive by? Or those cool shoes that person is wearing? All you'll have to do is look at it, and your mobile handset or AR (augmented reality) equipped eye-glasses will identify the object, look up the best price and retailer and with the voice command "buy it", it's your's!"

This future is all going to be about the way that humans can interact with computers. Digital technology will be everywhere, everything will be reducible to digital data, and will have been recorded and therefore become accessible. Instead of sitting in front of a PC or holding a tablet, computers will be built into everything around us and interaction will happen naturally. They will become "invisible tools which will blend into everyday life".

The next generation may never see a computer screen in the physical and formal way that has been used up till now. They will summon content and information on the go wherever and whenever they want it, they will organise and select from it in whichever way they want, they will send it to friends/colleagues by simple voice command or hand wave. As a result you won't even need to carry a mobile phone, you'll instead be able to access wifi or 4G or other networks and simply say a number or pick it off a called-up content sheet. News can be summoned and read via holographic display or on electronic paper and can be "dismissed" when no longer required. It will be an extraordinary new world and by 2020 we will already be seeing this sort of environment gaining critical mass.

Eras of Computing and Human Interaction

1990 to 2009 *Point and Click*

▼

2009 to 2012 *Touch 'n Go!*

▼

2012 to 2015 *Touch 'n Talk*

▼

2015 to 2018 *Command 'n Connect*

▼

2018 to 2020 *Think Talk Move*

Chapter 4:

Digital Transformation: key lessons and success factors

A recent MIT /Cap Gemini study showed that 79% of all execs interviewed felt that "digital transformation" should be a top 3 agenda item over next 3 years. But only 12% felt that their organisations had really seized this opportunity.

For most companies nowadays, digital transformation has so far been focussed externally. It's been about opening new channels to engage stakeholders and customers. It's been about setting up web sites, a mobile app, a Facebook page, a Twitter feed, perhaps some social media monitoring. Among B2C businesses there has also been a surge of development around e-commerce, finding new sources of revenue and growth.

These market-facing initiatives have often been successful. Large scale incumbents have begun to find their "digital feet" and are now major players in online commerce and customer engagement. The likes of Tesco.com, Bank of America, Procter & Gamble, Macys, Next, Starbucks, Burberry, Bradesco Bank, Direct Asia and many other consumer-facing businesses have adapted and responded to market pressures and competitive demands.

But, very few companies, whether B2C or B2B, have looked at how digital technology could also transform *internally* and impact *"the way they work"*.

There is in fact plenty of talk about this, conferences and seminars abound on the role of new technology solutions to transform a company. But that talk has *not yet* translated into any wide-scale corporate transformation. And this is being reflected in surveys like the MIT /Cap Gemini one. Most see the opportunity but few have yet truly grasped it.

Customer-facing web sites and initiatives are all good, and can clearly make a significant impact. They are also newsworthy and gain PR and shareholder interest. But many feel that the real digital opportunity lies more fundamentally in how the company is organised, the technologies it deploys, is it taking advantage of developments in the Cloud and Open Standards, how it can evolve to be more streamlined and cost-efficient, automate processes, move to self-serve, how it can take advantage of technology to find new ways of working that ultimately lead to more and longer term advantages in its markets.

Let's look at some examples; here are some organisations who are leaders in this digital transformation field:

(i) *Burberry*: Burberry truly began its investment in digital back in 2006. At that time, it took the obvious key steps around relaunching its web site. It also took some fundamental decisions and adopted some key "digital technology" principles. First of these was to establish a common platform. They could see limited value in allowing each country manager to build their own web operation. One platform, one approach, one global governance to manage and administer that. These guiding principles have really helped ensure that Burberry could move forward with digital technology in a fast, coherent and coordinated way, cutting out duplication and allowing a truly global presence to develop.

This way of doing business, this principle of how best to adopt technology innovation, then began to infiltrate inside the way the company operated, impacted its internal processes and ways of working. For example, product design became a fully digital process. Designs could be "shipped" digitally to suppliers and partners. People from all over the global Burberry community could input, share ideas, get engaged. Manufacturers had to comply and adapt to the Burberry way of working. Product development was not only more universal but the whole product cycle development time was substantially reduced.

Burberry have been on a digital journey that has now lasted more than 8 years. And it is still ongoing. The company is learning all the time what can be achieved, what typical roadblocks and obstacles it will likely encounter and how to move and adapt quickly. It has learnt that digital transformation cannot be viewed as one big change programme. The trick, the key lesson, is to look at this process by process. The goal is to identify a key process which could be improved by adopting a digital technology solution. Whether in product design, or in procurement, or in HR or in Finance, or in customer ordering or in in-store payment processing. Pick a process, pick an internal hero to champion the change.

Among other things Burberry also has established its own "Innovation Unit". This is an internal team whose task is to identify the next key process to undergo digital transformation and then prepare the groundswell of interest, support and identify the enabling technology which can drive the change and deliver the target benefits.

(ii) Nestlé: Nestlé made its decision to get serious about digital technology during 2010 following a PR disaster in its use of social media and Facebook particularly. Nestlé CEO Paul Bulcke made the key decision that digital is now mission critical for the company and "key to get it right!"

This led to a series of reviews and a new digital investment strategy developed. Among other things there was recognition that a lot could be learnt from the best digital players. There was an opportunity not just to learn from best practice but also to leapfrog competition. So links were established with the likes of Amazon, Google and Facebook and people sent out on fact-finding missions to learn how to take full advantage of developments in digital technology. A dedicated Silicon Valley team was set up to get close to these leading edge organisations and learn how to "co-innovate".

In addition a "digital acceleration" team was set up at Nestlé HQ. Employees apply for a 6 to 12 month secondment for intensive training, to establish common understanding and ways of working, to bring that back out to local markets to enable faster coordination and adoption. There are now even "satellite training centres" in China, Italy and other locations.

The overall goal is to establish new common shared global platforms, the ability to collaborate easily and efficiently, achieve the full benefits of scale from a global brand in its manufacturing, distribution and marketing, to implement new ways of working that incorporate digital technologies that can "permeate" the entire company.

One of Nestlé's key co-innovation partners has been Salesforce.com. While most companies will basically just buy the SFDC licence, Nestlé decided to establish with them a joint digital transformation leadership team. They established something closer to a business partnership rather than a vendor-customer relationship. There are joint teams, shared learning and know-how, the opportunity to develop together new IP and approaches which would be shared and a real commitment from Salesforce.com to see Nestlé emerge as one of its key customers and trophy case studies.

At the heart is the SFDC cloud /SaaS business model. But alongside that is a deep commitment to establish a single data platform that will give Nestlé a single global view of its B2B and potentially also its B2C customer data and enable insight that could drive better end-customer engagement, find new sources to sell-in the full product portfolio and new ways to generate revenue growth. The interest in getting this universal data view, to understand it and have the analytics capability to take advantage of it is seen as the key benefit.

(iii) *Hays*: Hays is a global recruitment company and in 2009 new CEO Alistair Cox embarked upon a full scale technology transformation programme. The goal was to utilise new advances in technology tools to establish a flexible, scalable and adaptable platform.

The idea of hiring a major IT consulting firm like an Accenture or Deloitte or Cap Gemini to conduct a 3 year IT review and implementation programme with hundreds of external consultants at vast expense was seen as an outdated and inappropriate way forward.

The principle, in contrast, was that things are moving so fast, that any IT investment needs to be flexible and responsive to change, quick and easy to implement and able to be replaced without major risk or substantial new cost requirements. "If we're going to be successful in the future then we need to have an infrastructure that allows us to plug things in. And we won't know now what all those future "plug-ins" will look like".

Hays set about replacing its entire IT stack with support from open standards being a key priority in software selection. And for example, Cloud-based solutions would also be encouraged.

Hays set up a process review team. Its task was to do a process map across each of the key steps in the company's value chain. The aim was to develop a roadmap that identified which process would be tackled when. The initial goal was to find one or two major processes that had immediate support for change and which could make a big impact. Those processes which were more complex or where the benefit of change was uncertain, those would be put in a stage 2 or stage 3 group. They could be tackled better at later stages of the company's digital transformation journey, for when the organisation had more learning, know-how and confidence on how to go about implementing and easily capturing the change benefits.

Hays chose key software tools according to these guiding principles. They chose "posting vacancies on job boards" as a key process. And they wanted to have that process simplified, totally automated to enable job board posting, search and selection in a totally automated manner for both employers and prospective employees. "Search is the heart of what we do, it's our core process and critical we could get that right and continue to adapt it as technology evolved". For this solution, Hays chose an Oracle Intelligence Enterprise solution as its data warehouse for reporting and analytics, an infrastructure deploying PeopleSoft, a recruitment software tool from Bond Adapt and a Google Search application. All this was built with a tailored user-interface enabling Hays people to conduct the searches they would find helpful. And each of these solutions, especially from Bond and of course from Google came with an open web standards approach. The whole platform was completely web-enabled so all information could be shared and easily distributed.

"Now we can focus on the user experience and we don't have to worry about the plumbing and infrastructure, that is all in place. Digital leadership in this company has been a joint exercise involving all functions and departments. It's been an especially strong collaboration between IT and Marketing. We have done all this digital change to gain one advantage: that is our ability to engage customers and get more growth. And we 've achieved that".

Overview of lessons learnt/ keys to success

There is now a still relatively small but growing list of companies who have made real progress with their digital transformation. From global multi-nationals like 3M, GE and Cisco to smaller niche market operators like Farrow & Ball paints, IC International yarns and threads, Norgren fluid controls manufacturing, Bobcat Doosan construction equipment, Eden Springs water coolers, Pitney Bowes printer /office supplies…

Importantly these companies are shaping or reshaping themselves to make sure they are winners and still winning by the end of this decade. They have made decisions to stop talking about the need for change and the potential for change, but are now taking the tougher steps of working out how to get there. It's getting started on this migration journey that's key, with a commitment to it, an investment plan to back it up and a vision of the end-game and benefits, the size of the prize!

There are a number of key lessons about how to best go about this:

(i) *Find an internal champion*: key is to have someone like a Chief Digital Officer, someone who can be the internal champion of digital change. It's important that this person is not simply from a market-facing eg e-commerce background.

- They need to be able to understand technology deeply.
- They also need to be able to understand key business processes and perhaps have some knowledge of process "re-engineering".
- Commercial savvy
- Outstanding cross-company relationship-building /stakeholder management skills
- They need to be well up-to-speed with new technology and innovation

  As it can be hard to find this combination of skills in one person, and given the scale and complexity that can accompany this change agenda, then some organisations are setting up a small central team that in combination has these skills and can work collaboratively to set the agenda and the priorities. That team might consist of the Chief Digital Officer, plus:

- Head of Programme Management
- Head of Technology Innovation
- People /Process /Culture officer

(ii) Define the size of the prize!

Right now today there may be no "burning platforms", the business may be moving forward and while growth may be slow, profits are holding up. In which case the inertia factor will kick in/ the "why-change" when things are going ok?

Of course this digital transformation opportunity is not intended as any short term fix or boost to this fiscal's numbers. It is much more about the long term, about being in a position to win in 3 or 5 year's time, about working now to secure the long term survival and success of the company. It's the inertia factor of course which did for the likes of Kodak and which has killed off traditional bricks n' clicks retailers from Circuit City to HMV. It's not that these companies and others did not anticipate the upcoming digital challenges, it's just that they kept plugging way with existing business and operating plans assuming that the impact would be much later and they would have more time.

If there is one lesson in this fast-moving technology age, it is that things will happen more quickly than forecast, not less! As one IT exec has put it: "this company has spent the past 25 years building its IT and processes, it's now got about 3 years to reinvent them or we just won't survive. It's not just about changing some of the technology; it's about changing the way we do business"

To help address and manage these issues, it's important that whoever is championing the digital transformation agenda, gets to define what is the size of the prize, what are the key benefits, what might be the longer term customer and growth prospects, what might be the RoI potential to justify the business case, why do it. Some organisations in response to this challenge are establishing a key metrics and dashboard, a way of tracking progress toward an end-game where significant benefits *are* realised.

(iii) *Integrated platform*: One key lesson that both Cisco and 3M have found is the need to build a single integrated data platform. Their aim is to build a common one stop view of all their customer activity. And ideally the aim is to make this seamless so that any function and department, whether Procurement, Finance or Sales can all access, contribute to and leverage that single unified customer history and record, no matter what the customer touchpoint, whether through call centre, sales team or direct and remotely online, or a combination of all. The benefit is not just a more impactful way of engaging with customers but it also can provide the customer with that single view of the company. So no matter what way *they* interact they will find common product, pricing, promotion and a real time updated understanding of their needs.

Retailers have been especially proactive in pushing down this path. To date, one retailer has stood out with the success it has achieved in this direction. And that is UK-based Aurora Fashion group. They own a number of well-known retail fashion brands and are now 6 years into their multi-channel single view of customer IT transformation. It works and has delivered constant and increasing improvement in margin, inventory management and most critically product line by product line, store by store revenue growth allied with a strong online sales effort.

Among other things, as their "digital champion" at the time Ish Patel has commented: "this approach has given us the data and the resulting analytical insight to better manage the business and maximise both sales and margin" And another champion of this approach, Pfizer, has also commented on the value and importance of this approach: "Our top priority was to build a digital hub that created a common set of platforms and pipes. We were able to create real value from uniting the data from different platforms and silos and finding common insights across stakeholders to deliver greater value to them. What we didn't want as we embarked along our digital transformation journey was to have 1000 flowers blooming. They might all look nice but it just eventually leads to confusion. We wanted one version, one approach, one set of rules, one view of our customers"

Summary and Conclusion

This is such a big topic that it's impossible to cover all the ground. So for the moment let's summarise with a couple of short key points:

(i) A brief overview and summary from Axa Insurance:

"At Axa it was a learning curve for all of us. We had to start somewhere and be prepared to make mistakes. But we began with a core process that involved parts of our business and our customers, that was claims handling. We set up blogs and surveys to test out ideas and alternative ways of working. We opened that dialog set to employees and selected customers. We set up workshops with external IT suppliers to see if they could help us, and we picked suppliers who were lean mean and agile themselves, not the bigger cumbersome consultancies. We devised a new way of working with data in the Cloud, self-serve, streamlined procedures, real time data capture, fast response commitments. Once we decided what to do and what we wanted to get from this change, then we were able to launch a first phase in just 4 months. It surprised us. It completely changed our own expectations of what we could achieve. Now we feel we can change anything!"

(ii) How to get things going, how to establish this major change culture around technology innovation:

Steering Committees are nothing new or innovative and many are not used well. But a key learning is that what works here is getting the whole organisation involved, not just one or two parts, pushing ahead with this transformation in integrated from, not in silos, developing some real momentum and not letting inertia creep in. Having this committee led, at least in the initial stages, by the CEO, involving colleagues from different geographies, departments and teams, managing the timetable, having full scale monthly reviews, setting clear targets and deliverables… all the well-known rules for success, but now making it happen in this demanding digital transformation context. That seems to be a key to success.

Chapter 5

Digital Transformation: "how-to" blueprint

Digital Transformation is one of today's hot topics. Most every organisation and business leader will talk about it. This, from David Jones, the CEO of global advertising agency Havas is typical:

> *"Digital is the way to go. In today's world, you need to have global ambitions, but there is a size and scale where rapid change becomes very difficult. My single biggest focus is digitising our business globally. We need to develop a culture and capability where we can adapt and move quickly. We will need to radically simplify our structure. That is number one because it is very easy to slow down if we stay traditional"*

The big challenge that every exec now faces is to convert the well-received rhetoric into meaningful change and action. A recent study by MIT identifies what it calls a "digital imperative": adopt new technologies and new ways of working or, they conclude, face competitive obsolescence.

MIT conducted a world-wide survey and found some surprising findings:

- 63% of business people interviewed said the pace of technology change in their organisation was slow, it "just lacked any sense of urgency"
- 62% said that digital transformation was just not on the CEO's agenda: "we keep talking about it, attending conferences, setting up internal teams, but it all comes back to change and investment and we keep being told there are other priorities"
- 68% said that where there is digital change then it was only focussed on external customer-facing initiatives around web sites and mobile apps and not around internal opportunities to improve efficiencies, to streamline, automate and speed up processes and ways of working.

In the last chapter we looked at 3 specific case study examples of how some organisations had already begun to deliver major achievements on their "DT" journey.

We looked at Burberry, Nestlé and Hays. It was clear that each had made a substantial commitment to digital technology-led change. Each saw itself as on a journey; a journey that would take not months but years. And because we live in a world where technology is right now evolving rapidly, then that journey might last for the next 10 years. What was clear to each was that they could not afford to ignore this "digital imperative". If they did want to succeed then the CEO and the senior team had to mobilise and galvanise the whole organisation. It had to start from the top, it had to be widely communicated and explained, it had to be incorporated into everyone's KPI. It had to become part of the "way of doing business".

Here are some great examples of companies that are taking DT to heart.

John Lewis: as everyone based in the UK will know, JL is one of the most successful UK corporations. A retail group that dominates consumer shopping in grocery, apparel and homeware, has delivered consistent year on year growth across all its key financial metrics and now sees revenues at close to $15bn and continued upward trends in margin and like-for-like sales. Their CIO Paul Coby has been leading this technology-led change.

Like many, he sees the role of the CIO as fundamentally more challenging. "New technology is coming at us on all sides". But Paul has led JL in a continuous wave of improvement and change. Over the past 5 years, great progress has been made in building online capabilities for customers. Customers now can experience a joined-up multi-channel environment which connects store to online to mobile to social media touchpoints and provides an integrated experience.

That will continue. "But we are now getting deep into optimising our back end too".

JL recognise that if they are to deliver constant continual innovation in how customers can do business easily, smartly, conveniently then all the order-processing, logistics, fulfilment, invoice payment systems and solutions need to match up. And it needs to work all the way through the supply chain involving buying and procurement teams and key supply partners. Third party partners need to be as signed up to digital transformation as JL are and need to be able to participate in the JL programme as well as being committed to adapting and changing themselves.

"Our goal now is to modernise our back end. That is the big challenge.

Many retail groups and other companies will have systems that are maybe 20 years old. That is stopping the organisation from adapting and moving quickly. We are now in the process of *ripping out* 50 or 60 legacy systems as a comprehensive redevelopment. We are building a new technology infrastructure. We are fundamentally engaged in architecting and engineering what an omni-channel business will look like"

Developing the capability to do this is not easy. Just to keep pace with technology and how it is evolving is challenging. It requires continuous knowledge-building about the opportunities, continued assessment of new tech tools and developments. It requires a detailed understanding of best practices and lessons learnt. Understanding what new tech can bring, what parts of the Cloud, Open Standards, mobile connectivity for example are relevant and provide advantage. Not every new tech of course is right or is appropriate.

For John Lewis to have reached the point where it has identified "the 50 or 60 legacy systems to be ripped out" then they will have necessarily gone through a radical and thorough review, developed the business case and justification, all cross-functional and business heads will need to have been consulted and engaged, the risks, the time frames, the RoI will all need to have been evaluated, reviewed and agreed. They will have defined roadmaps, priorities, skills, who to lead which work streams, what capabilities needed, what milestones and specific targets to set for each quarter, each half year, each year end which will cumulatively add up to the stated vision.

To enable such an exercise many in the past would have automatically turned to one of the big consultancy groups, an Accenture, a Cap Gemini, an IBM or others. They would have signed up to a 3-5 year programme of change with scores, even hundreds of consultants crawling over the company, costing substantial sums. And if history is anything to go by then many such big tech programmes will have disappointed, coming in over-budget, over time and under performance. (I always recall one of the Heads of UK Government Procurement addressing a conference of senior IT execs and announcing that 85% of all government IT projects over the past 10 years had failed to deliver as promised! He was castigating and provocative, demanding explanations and improvement!).

UniCredit: one of Europe's largest retail banking groups, with €6bn of operating income, headquartered in Milan and operating widely across 20 countries mainly in southern and eastern Europe. UniCredit suffered like many banks in the credit crunch downturn of 2008, but is emerging as one of the new winning financial institutions. In a recent McKinsey interview, their CEO, Paolo Cederle, discussed the digital transformation journey that he has initiated and led across the Bank over the past 4 years. He calls it their Business Integrated Solution and it's still very much an ongoing programme. The objective was to redesign the IT environment so it could provide seamless, integrated front and back office solutions that took advantage of new enabling technologies and would set the Bank up to be a "winner in 2020".

Most importantly, UniCredit recognised the need to develop a culture of "digital innovation" throughout the organisation: "innovation is core to us, it's about the continuous improvement of services to our customers and to develop a new way of banking that is smart and cost effective. The market demands it and our customers and shareholders expect it. We have a commitment to invest in the development of leading edge solutions. New technology will be our key enabler. Our goal is to specifically link our internal functions of Research, Technology, Product Development and Marketing to provide new products and services that will drive our growth and our profitability".

As an example, UniCredit is establishing a new central shared services environment for 2015, targeting reductions in cost, quicker times to bring new products to market, improved working practices, better working environment to enhance internal employee satisfaction and productivity and design a more compelling and lasting customer engagement and experience.

UniCredit has also set up separate stand-alone teams or "factories" as they call it who are dedicated to eg new product development, or groups focussed on just one key process such as credit card processing with the objective of designing and launching a new solution in that space.

They have articulated a 6 step mantra: *innovation>flexibility>agility>transparency>time to market>cost efficiency*.

"We are all about improving our flexibility and agility in how we work, be innovative in developing new quicker, more automated ways of working, speed up time to market and time to process customer interactions. This requires constant and close collaboration across the whole company, IT, Operations and Commercial. We can no longer afford to work in silos"

And in all this the role, structure and responsibility of IT is changing too. "IT staff still need and use their IT skills but they are not necessarily any longer a part of an IT organisation. The traditional org chart has had to be thrown away. Key IT managers are now often assigned to core projects and teams and may eg report to the Head of a Business Line. In our new credit card project we brought together Procurement, IT, Application development, Commercial,

Compliance, Fraud Management and Customer Support into one integrated dedicated project group who all reported together to the Commercial Dir. It was disruptive change. But we have learnt that if we really want to win with digital transformation then this is what we need to do".

UNICEF: this is the world's leading charity working for children in some of most impoverished countries, but that has not stopped them establishing a "Digital First" programme of technology-led change.

Laila Takeh was appointed Head of Digital for UNICEF. The remit was to lead the organisation's digital transformation with responsibility to work across teams and departments to establish more effective ways of collaborating and working. "We recognised we need to become organisationally joined-up and could see how new digital technology tools could help us do that". They identified immediate improvements in ways to share data in real time, to collaborate more easily on projects no matter that key team members were in different parts of the world, join in key partners and stakeholders more seamlessly into various fundraising projects and initiatives.

"We needed to educate ourselves and learn and develop a broad understanding of technology as a group so that we could jointly design and improve how we did things. In a cross-organisation" environment we needed to develop the communication tools and processes at all levels to enable us to do this".

Laila has initiated several key things:

- "a digital hub", a group at the centre under her leadership who are champions of digital expertise, new technology options and this "digital first" change programme.
- an emphasis on better ways to communicate among internal teams using digital collaboration tools like Basecamp, Google Docs, wikis and internal social platforms like Yammer
- dedicate resource to staying up-to-date on technology and change improvement options
- develop a shared vision of how everyone would like the organisation to be; then work back to today and develop a roadmap of how to get there, how to reach that vision. "it may take years but we need to start somewhere"
- pick small steps first, "we decided to make a series of little bets"
- establish a culture where it's ok to make mistakes, "we can learn from our failures as well as our mistakes. From small wins and little failures we will

find unexpected strategies and tactics that lead to big and extraordinary impact"

"if we had to sum up, our "digital first" is all about the appropriate use of digital technology to enhance the experience, increase engagement [and funding] and reduce overhead."

Barclays and Sainsbury's: Both these companies provide a good example of an alternative approach to digital transformation.

While they have both embarked on their own internal digital transformation programmes, they have recognised that delivering change and improvement will inevitably take time. Like John Lewis, they are having to identify the 50 or 60 + core legacy processes and systems that need to be "ripped out". And the change time required to do that is considerable while still managing risk and delivering uninterrupted continuity to customer service and the organisation generally.

That internal programme needs to happen. But are there other ways to take advantage of this digital world and use new technology advances to build new capabilities and solutions?

The model for Barclays and Sainsbury's is to establish a separate stand-alone joint ventures unit. They have set up a dedicated team with its own space, place, culture and the freedom to build and establish its own technology platform. They have looked to create something which is as close to a "dot com" style entrepreneurial unit as possible. Fully backed, invested in but without the encumbrance of large international matrix organisation system and procedure checks and reviews, without the hierarchy of numerous sign-offs and approval stages, without a bureaucracy that would otherwise stifle creativity and innovation. They have the freedom to move quickly, flexibly and with agility, hire people with appropriate digital skills and entrepreneurial attitudes, pay market rates for the right people, use Open Standard software rather than eg Microsoft dot net, partner with Cloud providers rather than trying to justify doing it all in-house, deliver new products to markets in weeks rather than years, and do so at potentially a fraction of the cost.

The idea at one level is just to recognise that there are now new ways of doing business, of building a company, that trying to do that inside a large organisation is difficult and so why not set up NewCo and give it its head? Other companies are also looking at similar initiatives and ask the question: if we were setting up this company today then how would we do it? For sure we would not build the same technology and process that we have today, it would likely be very different, so why not try that, see what it looks like? It may become our future. It may show us how to do things and NewCo may become the vehicle for how we do business. We may even end up migrating all our customers onto the NewCo platform, replacing and winding-down our existing legacy environment.

★★★★★

These case examples illustrate just how fundamental a world of change we are living through and just how deep companies need to go to take advantage of the digital transformation opportunity.

A recent McKinsey study tried to answer the question: is this change worthwhile, can it deliver a strong RoI, it's one of the most challenging change agendas a company can face, so given all the restructuring required, is it likely to pay back?

On average McKinsey found that "digital transformation can boost the bottom line by more than 50% over the next 5 years for companies that pull all the key digital technology and change levers. This is driven especially by building new ways to engage with customers but also about shifting customer interactions to digital self-serve channels and automating resource or paper-heavy processes… digital is providing the opportunity to reshape the economics of competition across all key sectors".

This study, as well as one from MIT, have identified 7 core basic steps that a company needs to take before embarking on digital transformation:

1. *Estimate the value at stake*. It will vary by sector and by market, but what is the potential size of the prize? To do this, estimates can be made on the size of the digital sales potential and the cost reduction opportunities available. These two strands – sales and cost – may need to be considered independently. While sales revenues may come from market-placed activity, web and mobile engagement, those sort of initiatives by themselves will not necessarily lead to a lower cost to serve. That needs to be thought about as a separate opportunity in its own right. In the same way that John Lewis have a front end and separate though of course complimentary back-end programme.
2. *Prioritise*: no organisation can do this all at once; pick some early wins that look easier to achieve, the "little bets".

3. *Be ready to make some mistakes*: as UNICEF point out that might be the only way to learn how best to do things and what to avoid.

4. *Secure C-Level sponsorship* and active support. Research generally shows that still the majority of execs say digital change is too slow and suffers from lack of senior involvement.

5. *Establish a Chief Digital Officer*: this is someone who can be the champion of change. This person is the necessary expert on best practices, on what new tech tools need to be seriously evaluated and considered, what's out there in the Cloud that can be trusted and might accelerate things. This person ideally sits at the senior exec /Board table, asks the difficult questions about where are we on now on the DT change programme, is the voice of digital activation and opportunity, establishes the key metrics and milestones, reports on progress, evaluates competitor and other initiatives and makes sure digital learning is proactively shared and embraced.

   It's not an easy role, to be the voice of change and challenge and disruption. Vanguard companies in this space have learnt too that it can't be a lonely role. No good having it stuck in the back office with one person occasionally wheeled out to satisfy demanding shareholders. Much better to be a small but deliberately high profile team. Based at the centre and with counterparts in all the key business lines and geographies and departments. A virtual perhaps but unified group with a shared mission and purpose which starts from the top of the organisation.

6. *Education and learning*: to be successful companies need to cascade digital know-how and best practices throughout the organisation. It is as relevant to the most junior assistant as it is to the most senior team leader. This is where HR can step in to provide that means to learn. It may be through simple internal social networks or more formal e-Learning programmes, it may be through softer culture development or through establishing new individual performance measures and incentives, but it's essential to build up the drive for digital change and recognition of its potential bottom-up through the company.

7. *Identify key skill gaps:* This is a brave new world, it requires a readiness to change, a desire to learn new ways of working, a willingness and aptitude for embracing technology and becoming technically literate, a confidence that in abandoning traditional ways of working that new more effective and ultimately more satisfying solutions will be found.

Not everyone is up for that. And as DT takes hold so it might be necessary to reskill or reorganise and restructure. One skill set that companies often lack is Programme Managers with the required skills and experience. Success or failure will likely hinge on just how good a Programme Director or Manager is in leading the defined change work stream. That person needs core project management skills and disciplines, but also needs to be at minimum technically proficient and at best technically strong so they can engage and interact with confidence and with authority with the IT team. They also need to have exceptional senior stakeholder management skills to get continuous support for the cross-functional, cross-country changes that are needed. And ideally all this in a digital learning environment and ideally with a relevant track record of success!

Such people do exist! But are not easy to find. Companies need to evaluate the benefit of having such people, the value they can bring and what is the right level of pay and compensation that will attract and reward.

★★★★★

Digital transformation is set to be the major catalyst for change over the rest of this decade. A number of companies are now starting to set a 2020 vision and target, recognising that DT will represent their major opportunity for profitable growth over coming years. There's enough research and learning that shows this way forward is no longer an option, it's become a necessity, a "digital imperative" for survival and success. Few organisations today would argue against this "imperative", but the immediate challenge now is about converting the ideas into realistic and achievable change programmes that do deliver that winning position 2020.

Chapter 6

What is the HR impact of digital on future talent needs and hiring?

To what extent is digital changing the type of candidate that organisations are looking for? Has the arrival of this digital technology and multi-channel world changed the underlying characteristics and attributes of a successful modern day hire? Have we reached a sea-change in the type of skills, attitude and outlook that it takes to succeed?

Certainly right now there is a wide-spread view that it is hard to find good "digital" people. In a recent survey by e-Consultancy, 68% of HR professionals said they had difficulty recruiting staff who were sufficiently knowledgeable about digital technology and communications. 73% commented that digital was making a significant impact on preferred candidate profiles and 43% commented on the challenge of keeping up to date with the new digital trends and tools. What's more HR teams are having themselves to become increasingly "digitally savvy". 74% said they had had to become skilled in using online search tools to find out about a candidate's reputation and 46% said they had rejected a candidate based on what they had discovered about a person online with Facebook, YouTube and blogs being cited as key influences.

And it does look as though digital is making a substantial impact in the way companies generally do organise and go to market. A recent study by BCG (Boston Consulting Group) together with Google showed that the "digital economy" is already worth more than 7% of UK GDP at more than £100bn. That makes it larger than the construction, utilities and transportation sectors! And it is fast growing, expected to double over the next 5 years. At that level it will be larger than the UK Financial Services sector. In fact the UK is emerging as a global leader in this area. It has the largest internet sector in terms of absolute billions of GDP and e-commerce spend per household is higher than anywhere else in the world!

Among the many challenges that digital poses is that it is nevertheless relatively new and immature. It only started hitting the headlines not much more than a decade ago when we witnessed the first internet bubble during '98/ '99 and 2000. When that all crashed, many internet businesses were closed and teams disbanded. It took a further 5 years till 2005 for the "Web 2.0" reawakening to occur and for companies to begin to see the power of the Net in terms of customer reach and business development. With that came a surge of interest in starting to ask for candidates who "got digital", who understood at least some of this new world and who could help navigate a way through this digital maze.

The need was especially strong in marketing and technology. The rapid rise of online sales and information provision meant there was an immediate need for tech people who could design, build, optimise and maintain web sites and for marketing people who could use and deploy e-commerce know-how to maximise site traffic and effectively deliver high sales conversion rates. And those needs have not gone away, they have in fact now become far more complex.

"Digital" is a widely used term but it is a catch-all umbrella for a whole range of different skills and requirements. For example within "digital marketing" there are a large number of specialist skills. These include: Search engine marketing, search engine optimisation, affiliate marketing, web analytics, campaign analysis, creative marketing, brand strategy development, customer retention, eCRM, email marketing, and now add on mobile commerce, social media and interactive TV. All these areas are unique and distinctive skill sets. They all require a candidate with specific know-how and skills. But if a business team asks for a "digital marketeer", there is often the assumption that someone with knowledge of the online world can turn their hand to any and all of these very different things. And yet what can make a difference is a candidate who really is for example, steeped and immersed in mobile, who really does have the case studies and the war stories and the lessons learnt so that they know intuitively what will drive successful mobile comms, content and commerce.

The same can be said for the technology area. In a recent survey by IBM of 2000 IT professionals, 91% said that digital technology tools would dominate and would form the primary IT delivery model. They mentioned a wide range of skill set requirements from IT visioning and enterprise architecture, through to SOA (service-oriented architecture) and SaaS (software as a service) and Cloud computing. The IT community are also placing a much higher emphasis on Programme Management and delivery recognising that the migration to a new digital technology environment will likely need transformational change across geography and business units and will need expert tech and commercial change and delivery skills. There are also core and specialist skill requirements around IT infrastructure, data centres, data protection and security, MIS (management information services), social networks, mobile, voice recognition, content management, "green IT" and the multitude of different software programming skills from Dot Net to Java to Open Source experience to HTML5 and so on…

It's a challenging environment, it's new and there are no real proven solutions. Businesses are forced to learn and experiment as they go and make a bet, however reasoned, on what are the core skills and needs to help drive the future success and growth of the organisation. And that is often why job specs for "digital" jobs are difficult to write. Unlike for example a search for a new financial controller where there are many years of understanding and experience as to the sort of qualifications and experience required. Digital expertise is harder to define and describe. What are the right qualifications, what sort of university degree is most relevant, how evaluate years of hands-on experience, how valuable is someone who is steeped in IT generally versus a new grad who has grown up using and learning the new digital tools and environment? If there's a need for a marketer then how transferable are for example search engine marketing skills into a more general online marketing remit? If looking for a new architect how familiar and expert do they need to be in cloud computing, if according to IBM, that will be the specific area that will dominate IT development for the rest of this decade?

In summary there are probably 5 key things that can be identified from all the research and experience that distinguish a candidate who is best-suited for the digital world. The focus here is less on the specific skills eg in Search engine marketing specialisation or in SOA, but more around the qualitative attributes that mark out an individual. What is the "right stuff" that HR teams and business owners should be looking for? It's all changing so fast and hard to know what will be required in the business in 12 months time, let alone 3 years out. But can we put together a simple and sustainable check-list of core attributes and characteristics?

The 5 keys are:

1. *A restless spirit*
2. *Comfort and confident with technology (but not necessarily a "techie")*
3. *Communication and interpersonal skills*
4. *Self-sufficiency*
5. *An appreciation that it's a multi-channel world*

A restless spirit: this is someone who enjoys and relishes change! It's the individual who is happy that there is no complete job spec, who is comfortable that there is no clearly defined box for the role, it's that person who recognises that we are going through a revolution in communications and in technology and who wants to be part of that, contributing to it, challenging traditions and accepted methodologies and processes, a force for change who is unhappy if things are status quo or if things take too long to happen, an inquisitive mind who wants to know about the latest technologies and tools and is passionate about them.

Comfort and confident with technology: this is a vital prerequisite. They need not necessarily have a deep tech background if they are for example up for a marketing role, but they must have an appreciation of it, a desire to understand it and ability to talk about it. They need to know what is "cloud computing", why it's being so widely discussed and be able to see the potential commercial applications. They need to appreciate that doing something in mobile for example is not just about "creating an app for the iPhone" but that there are scores of other handsets which need to be separately managed and that configuration of the online site may require significant technical resource. They need to be a point of contact that can translate tech advances into commercial feasibility

Communication and Interpersonal skills: a recent survey by the US Center for Public Education highlighted this area as the key requirement. "The 21st Century is bringing a requirement for new skills and tools in the workspace. Strong interpersonal skills for collaboration and communication will be a "must-have" competency. It's the power to interact effectively, to communicate both face-to-face, in large and small meetings, both verbally and with data, to relate well to others and to cooperate with them, to negotiate and manage potential conflicts of priority between departments and to lead through persuasion. In times of change and especially where organisations are having to adopt new technologies and new ways of working, this is going to be a core skill".

Self sufficiency: organisations are already moving toward remote working environments. The concept of everyone travelling to an office to do a day's work and do that every day of the week is a not a 21st century way of working. Unilever for example have adopted a workplace strategy which looks at three categories of employee. They call it "resident, mobile and offsite". Residents are still those who come to work and have their own desk and workspace. That might be eg the office manager, security staff as well as others who prefer that style. The Mobile worker has typically been the salesperson out and about with customers but returning to base and hot-desking there, so having access but no "permanent home". And then the Remote worker, who may never visit the office, may be established at home or be a connected contractor or consultant or supplier who needs and gets access to fellow employees, office news and information, email etc but always from a remote station.

Unilever are also studying how the next 5 years will further change that categorisation. One thing they are certain about: there will still be a need for an office, but there will be a substantial shift from resident to mobile and offsite. This has far-reaching impact on people. Are they the sort that can cope with this change in work pattern? Are they self-sufficient in that they could be set up to eg work from home? Are they reliable in that they may have limited physical contact with colleagues and it will be harder to monitor their performance?

Appreciation it's a multi-channel world: while this has all been about digital, it is just as important for good candidates to appreciate that there is much that is not digital. 20% of the UK population are not online, e-commerce accounts for some 15% to 20% plus of total retail and while many will research online still the majority will shop and buy in-store. TV advertising still accounts for some 40% of all advertising spend and is still the key way for any organisation wishing to build a mass wide-reaching consumer brand. 26% of consumers have smart phones with Net access but that's still a large majority that do not and most people today will shop and research and interact in a multi-channel and cross platform way. So it's critical that good marketers and technology people do appreciate this, do understand that you can't just "switch off analogue" overnight, that the spread of online and digital technology will still be unfolding for the rest of this decade and that any business solution will need to accommodate customers wherever they are and through whatever channel they choose to interact.

★★★★★

It's always been a challenge of course to find the best candidates for the organisation. There will always be competition for the very best people and a premium on their time and services. But as we look at the next few years it is clear that digital is placing an added layer of complexity. There are many people who will claim to be "digital experts" and cite years of experience, but the facts are that that whole world has emerged so very recently that there just are not that many experts around. Social Media and Mobile only really got going a few years ago. So claims of "many" years of expertise in those areas need to be carefully examined. Equally there has been talk about SaaS and Cloud but few organisations and people have any genuine and immersed expertise and insight. And this shortage of really experienced talent puts a bigger emphasis on the 5 keys discussed here: to find those individuals with the spirit, the confidence, the interpersonal skills, the self-sufficiency and the strategic multi-channel awareness that they can operate effectively in this digital world and make the outstanding impact that they've been hired for.

Chapter 7

5 keys to finding the best digital talent

Digital has now of course become part of every successful organisation's DNA. It has developed rapidly and offers new ways of working, quicker and more cost-effective solutions as well as providing new routes to customers and markets. It's become an engine of change as well as revenue growth and vanguard companies are experiencing substantial upsides in business.

At the same time, this catalyst for change is still a relatively new phenomenon and it means that the talent pool that has real depth of experience and expertise and know-how is relatively limited. Some companies are now saying that it is becoming very hard for them to find good "digital" talent; that they are struggling to support and develop the growth opportunities because they cannot get the right people into their teams.

But the most successful companies do not seem to find this same problem. Those who get digital, who fully embrace it from the CEO and HR to the most junior assistant, those for whom it has become their way of working and the source of growth as well as saving cost, those where there is real commitment, investment and priority behind their digital transformation programs, those are the companies that have also learned how to build a really simple but very effective digital talent-finding and recruiting model. This now looks at those best practices.

One immediate observation is that these "best practices" are far from being rocket science. In many ways they are nothing new, they are no more than what good talent finding processes should anyway be all about. But in these days when the "digital talent pool" is still growing and when there is very high demand for the best people, then these "better processes" and practices become all the more compelling.

1. The Senior management team buys into the essence of Digital as their key driver.

How many times do candidates ask this… does the management team at senior level really get this, are they paying lip service to digital technology, to Cloud and web and e-commerce and mobile, or is this centre stage of their investment strategy? Good candidates say they repeatedly come across organisations who say they want to change, to embrace these new opportunities, but who in practice are doing very little that's different.

And candidates have wised up to this. It's one of their first questions. How important is this to the Board, how critical is this to the company's agenda, what levels of budget and support will be available? How often do candidates go to an interview and ask these leading questions, only to be disappointed and frustrated by the answer. They discover that in fact they will be in effect a "lone wolf", relegated to being a "voice of influence" (sometimes euphemistically described as a "champion of change"), that there will be no team to support them, that "this year there is very little budget, but next year... "

The best candidates will not be fooled. They will have been through these foundation experiences, they will have seen the pitfalls and frustrations. They will be looking for a place where they *can* make an impact and effect change.

Needless to say those organisations who want to do something but who don't back up the words with substantive commitments will not attract and get the best people.

2. Acknowledging that this need for digital-led change is now urgent and that all is not perfect!

Many companies are relatively weak in their digital know-how today, their IT legacy systems are poor and unsuited to new ways of working, their online environment is not optimised for the user experience and concepts of fundamental IT innovation are discussed but rarely pursued.

Yet in candidate interviews, it's as though there's a big cover-up. Instead of acknowledging the weaknesses or better put, "the opportunities for change", the interview is more about joining the team, fitting-in with existing work patterns, joining the culture, about gentle evolution when sometime more progressive and radical action is required.

But, the best digital talent is usually passionate about what can be done, big believers in what new technology solutions can achieve and wants to find an environment where they can practice what is preached. And be able to do so with immediate effect. As soon as they sense an organisation is slow or reluctant then once again they will themselves be very hesitant about joining such a culture.

3. A fast recruitment process

Good candidates respond positively and enthusiastically when the company also operates in that same way. From brief to first contact to final interview the process should take just a few weeks. It should not take months. And unfortunately months is the timeframe that many, often apparently very sophisticated large companies, will operate in. How many times does a business /function leader give out a brief, only for it then to stall while others sign-off, and then the key interviewer is busy or travelling or away, and then several weeks go by after the first interview before the second interview is set-up and then similar long gaps, and while for the candidate this process is potentially very much the centre of their whole world as they contemplate what for them is a big career move, this same sense of priority, of importance, of care and concern is often just not mirrored by the interviewing company.

Disillusion can quickly set in as the candidates starts to question: is this role really important to the company, are they committed to this new venture /initiative, they might be giving me good feedback but do they really want to make this hire, why do I have to wait weeks to hear if there is going to be a next step.

These delays should be the exception, but in practice they are common. Suffice to say that in this "war for good digital talent" those who interview quickly and positively get the best people.

4. Some salary/ comp. flexibility

Because "digital" is new, because the talent pool is limited, because things are changing fast, then to maximise recruitment success, the learning is the need for at least some salary /comp. package flexibility.

Of course it's understood by candidates that the company will have salary bands at different levels in the company, that the compensation needs to approximately match up to peers, and that the new digital exec cannot be too much out of line.

But the fact is that there is a premium on salary levels for the best talent. That the best people will be paid well, that if it comes to making an offer, then the best out of this limited talent pool might just justify a premium to the base pay, or some kind of "sign-on" signature, or some higher grant of options or some inducement that does reflect their worth in the market.

It sometimes happens that a candidate will turn down job opportunities for roles they would be brilliant for simply because at the final negotiation the salary offered was below expectations or was less than that from a more progressive rival company.

Why is it that Google, Apple, Amazon and eBay are regarded as having the best digital talent today? One reason is that they did not compromise in paying the best salary levels to attract the top talent. Their mantra is: "the best companies should attract the best people". It might have been regarded as a significant investment in their early days to pay high compensation levels but they argue that that investment has more than paid back with their continued streams of market-leading innovations.

5. Measure how effective the recruitment process is /where it can be improved

There are certain key metrics which enable an organisation to measure how effective it is at finding and recruiting the best people:

- average time a job role is open
- ave. number of candidates interviewed per role
- ave. number of interviews a candidate has
- time from brief to offer
- % offers accepted
- ave. salary premium if any
- time from brief to candidate starting
- ave. length of time new hire stays with the company
- % who stay > 2 years

This dashboard /scorecard, combined with other metrics key to a specific organisation, can be kept and monitored. It may just highlight where things can be improved!

★★★★★

Finally, let's acknowledge that there are many brilliant people out there but they don't all need to be a rockstars to make a superb contribution

Recent work by a combined HR team from Caterpillar, General Mills and Schlumberger showed that a key delaying factor in recruitment was being too idealistic and setting unrealistic expectations of the profile and required abilities in the job description and brief.

The research showed that briefs often set out a "wish list" of desired attributes and expertise. And it concluded that often times no candidate could realistically be expected to match that wish list! It also showed that against those search criteria the level of salary offered often just would not be enough to attract that sort of person anyway.

So companies will frequently set off down a path where it will be very hard to find the right match. Hence there is delay and frustration with the process. The recommendation from the research is, put simply, be realistic!

There are many talented people out there who will do a very good, honest and often a tremendous job, but they are not all rockstars! They don't all walk on water! And do they need to, to do this particular job really well?

"Hire people with potential, give them the opportunity to spread their wings, put the right compensation behind them, watch them fly"
> Jack Welch, previous CEO of GE

"It's not about the coffee, it's about the people and growing and nurturing and teaching then so they can fulfil their potential"
> Howard Behar, founder of Starbucks

"Get the team together, only then can you make something happen"
> Thomas Watson, former President of IBM

Chapter 8

How the workplace will change and the workforce will need to adapt

What will be the impact of digital transformation on the 2020 workplace? Will office life still be more or less the same, will we still have an office to go to, will we all need to become tech geeks and programmers, will be still be typing on Microsoft Word or will be talking to our computer and using VRS, will we still meet and socialise with our co-workers and have office friends and networks or we simply interact remotely, how global will be our remit or will we still act and think within local country boundaries, will there still be specific function groups eg for Marketing and IT or will we all need to become multi-skilled, multi-channel experts?

For sure, the workplace will have changed and there are 7 key themes that will characterise this change:

1. Mobile: meaning same speed instant screen access from anywhere
2. Anytime: 24/7/365 communication
3. Democratisation: more people involved
4. Flatter hierarchies: less emphasis on managing downwards/upwards and more on contribution and engagement
5. The "Knowledge worker"
6. Global: no boundaries
7. Automation: a lot of what we do today will be done automatically by machines.

Let's consider each of these:

1. Mobile: At Unilever, as in most every other organisation, the culture and expectation used to be that people would come to work. They would clock-in or register or at least make their presence felt and be available. Today, Unilever's policy has shifted to accommodate three types of employee. What they call: resident, mobile and offsite. Residents are still those who come to work and have their own desk and workspace. That might be the Office manager, security staff as well as others who prefer that style. The Mobile worker has typically been the Salesperson out and about with customers but returning to base and hot-desking there, so having access but no "permanent home". And then the remote worker, who may never visit the office, may be established at home or be a connected contractor or consultant or supplier who needs and gets access to fellow employees, office news and information, email etc but always from a remote station.

While that may be a simple but very appropriate way to think about the workplace today, Unilever also are studying how the next 10 years will change that categorisation. One thing they are certain about: there will still be a need for an office, but there will be a substantial shift from resident to mobile and offsite. This has far-reaching impact on the size and amount of office space required. It also and most especially impacts the IT and communications systems that must enable people to still work effectively in teams and make informed and pragmatic decisions while perhaps never meeting in person.

"The challenge we have is that most of our employees do like coming to work, they enjoy the learning and stimulation of working with colleagues as well as the social interaction. The advent of digital technology allows us to find new ways of working and collaborating but they will also require us to get used to a different type of "office life".

So the trend to mobile and offsite will continue to grow, it may be driven as much by pressures to continue to reduce costs as by the availability of technology and what it can easily enable. One stark message here for the commercial property industry: will we still need the same amount of office space in 2020? Surely, companies will be reviewing just how many people they really do need to house in the future. If a persuasive business and HR case can be made for encouraging mobile and offsite then it will be accompanied by the need for fewer square feet. That might impact the major business centres less than the secondary ones. Companies might still feel they "need a presence in the City" for example, but business parks in secondary and tertiary locations may well struggle to retain occupancy rates.

This physical space dilemma is no different than the one discussed facing retail organisations. As online shopping becomes more and more attractive and easy, retailers will need fewer shops. And only now after years of the "doom mongers" saying that there is a real estate time bomb waiting to go off, are retailers truly beginning to review their shop portfolio and space needs over the next 10 years. Such are the leadtimes that it can easily take up to 10 years from design to build to occupancy. If the future does require less physical office space then it may soon be time to sell stock in commercial property developers!

2. Anytime: The ubiquity of computers and mobile devices will increase expectations of immediate interaction and response. Consumers already expect 24/7/365 access to the internet, to online shopping (ever seen a web site notice saying closed for the weekend!), to call centres, to get technical support whenever needed, access to bank accounts and money transfers, the availability of advice and service when they want it and wherever they are. As that consumer demand continues to grow, all forms of customer service will need to provide round the clock support. Gone will be the days that people will accept "our office hours are open 9 to 5 Monday till Friday".

Metro Bank is just one of the new organisations to recognise this. It has been a pioneer in retail banking offering 7 day week branch opening hours 8 till 8. Will we for example see other financial institutions follow? Most have now recovered from the banking crisis but have frustratingly reverted to their old ways, shored up by recovering profits. No need or urgency to change just yet? But expect continued customer demand and pressure for convenience to continue to drive retail and banking innovation. And if these changes follow through, they may become part of a universal trend to offer a continuous "we never close" service and facility.

And all that means that the workforce will need to adapt to that pattern. It's already happened in retail where some stores open 24 hours and of course the Manufacturing sector, with its high fixed cost asset base, has long ago implemented 24/7 shift patterns and working practices to leverage that cost base and investment.

In today's world of competitiveness, the end of the "job for life" philosophy, cost and other pressures, few jobs are truly "safe" and the workforce has had to become more adaptable and flexible to keep its jobs and its wages. So accepting shift patterns, having a willingness to work "nights" while having the day off, participating in global teams and ventures which may conflict with historic social /relaxation at home with family patterns, may become more widely adopted and accepted as the normal way of doing business and holding down a job. In fact most managers today, especially if they are involved in a global company, find they have to have a huge amount of 24/7 flexibility. Time zones mean that a US company dealing with a partner organisation or with colleagues working in China has only a limited window of same day time to set up video and conference calls. The need to often just do that means that if a manager in San Francisco wanted to speak to a colleague in Shanghai on the same day then that call would have to be no later realistically than 06.00 PST, as the time in Shanghai at 16 hours ahead would be 22.00. And it's becoming increasingly common for execs who want to have a "quiet chat" with a colleague or investor or recruit away from the rush of the day job, to book conference calls during the weekend.

A Gartner report looking at the 2020 workplace makes this prediction: "many employees will have neither a company-provided physical office nor a desk and their work will increasingly happen 24 hours a day, seven days a week. This will create issues as the lines between personal, professional, social and family matters will disappear"

3. Democratisation: A recent McKinsey report on Web 2.0 found that companies who actively encourage wide-spread internal and social networking were more successful than those that did not. The report identified twelve specific web networking technology tools which could contribute to make that difference. These included: *blogs, mash-ups (applications that eg combine multiple sources of data into a single tool), microblogging, peer to peer, podcasts, prediction markets ("the wisdom of crowds"), rating, RSS (Really Simple Syndication), social networking, tagging, video sharing, and wikis.*

And encouraging this internal sharing and discussion and collaboration and keep up to date communication was found to produce benefits in a number of areas. Increased employee satisfaction was near the top of the list as employees were discovering new ways to contribute and feel part of a community with a shared purpose. And the company found benefits in reduced operating costs and an increasing number of successful innovations to the working practices resulting in increased speed of decision-making and faster time to market.

Sounds like this is the way all companies should be moving. A demonstrable and proven way to make a company work in a digital environment. Benefits to both employee and employer. Potentially easy to implement even though many companies struggle without a unified messaging and collaboration platform, disparate systems, no connected-up intranet, firewalls or policies restricting access to the world wide web or to social networks specifically. But at the end of the day they don't need much more than a web browser and a password protected environment. And there are companies who are already out there and making this Web 2.0 internal socialising work.

Dresdner Bank uses an internal knowledge-sharing "socialtext wiki" to manage meeting agendas and capture the key points and conclusions to provide an easily accessible record and archive trail of project progress open to all. Dell has an active social networking programme that reaches out to customers but also seeks to engage internally to help unify a geographically diverse global work force. And instead of waiting for the next CEO podcast, everyone is encouraged to blog, set up their own community groups whether work-related or not and to participate in discussion forums. Walt Disney, Oracle/ Sun Microsystems and even General Motors are finding these techniques valuable in both communicating their own corporate messages but also giving everyone in the company a voice and most importantly a channel to be heard.

This is the digital equivalent of the water cooler conversation. It's been heralded as one of the biggest changes in a century in the way companies organise and communicate internally. While much was made of the intranet, it did typically rely on corporate IT to establish some unnecessarily complex solution which took 2 years to build, cost millions, didn't work well, had an appalling user interface and noone used. This time around web technology makes it easy, the interface can be simple, Facebook can be the template, keep it hosted in the cloud, adopt a standard keyword search facility and let the users populate and paint the space. As a recent piece of Forrester research on the subject commented: "the product or process is owned by all the people who create it, wherever they are in the creation process, it drives a collective sense of ownership and responsibility".

4. Flatter hierarchies: today's classic hierarchical organisation structure is not fit for the 2020 work place. The new technology world and the tech socials who will drive it will require a more collaborative and cooperative way of working. "Command and Control" hierarchy will need to give way to "Autonomy and Empowerment". Looser team-based designs will need to be adopted that replace today's multi-layered approach where we often find managers managing managers!

As Charles Handy, one of the great strategists of recent times has pointed out: "there is no logic which says that the sequence of decision-making needs to be turned into a vertical ladder so that those who make the early decisions are higher up in the hierarchy than those who implement them. And as history has shown, the larger the organisation the more complex the hierarchy and the greater the bureaucracy".

"Destructured" organisation design is now being recognised as a form more suited to a fast-paced competitive environment which needs to be able to adapt quickly, make more immediate decisions and better harness the skills and expertise of the *whole* workforce. The buzz words are all about "flexibility, speed, integration and innovation". And the magic number is 50.

50 is regarded as the size of structure and team where everyone can know everyone else, where it's possible to establish critical mass in terms of the variety of skills and experience, where people can easily communicate and collaborate, where decision-making can be quick, where "office politics" can be kept to a minimum and where a true sense of collective ownership can be fostered. Structure can be kept to small teams and team leaders where there is less emphasis on managing and more on doing and contributing. This can generate a sense of empowerment and a feeling that each person is responsible. It's no longer about "I did my bit", but more about "this is mine and we've all got to get it right!"

And yes, this may sound somewhat utopian and the many who are involved today in a large corporate with all its established structures and ways of working may wonder how it is possible to migrate from the current to the new. But the forces for change will come both externally from the market place and the need to be competitive but also internally from the new generation of the workforce who will be making their own imprint on how they work and how best to organise.

HP, Xerox, General Electric are example of big companies who have nevertheless been pioneers of flatter structures. GE was the archetype of the top-down, command-and-control structured company. But they have found ways to re-design their structure so that the divisions run as smaller entrepreneurial units. One of their techniques was to introduce the term "boundaryless management". This was a direct and persistent attack on their traditional vertical structure. Siemens, before restructuring had 12 layers of management. After restructuring, it had considerably fewer. By proceeding cautiously, it managed its transition in a way that still protected the company's reputation as a good employer. Edward Jones, the US stockbroker, moved to make itself a flat company by structuring as a confederation of autonomous entrepreneurial units. They are nevertheless still bound together by a central set of shared core values and service ethics. The company today is a network of brokers, each of whom works from their own remote but connected office. Companies like Apple and Google are leaders among the new wave who have built their foundations on these same principles. It is becoming the preferred way of working for the new breed of tech companies who have the flexibility and agility to embrace digital technology in this changing landscape.

5. The Knowledge worker: The great business guru Peter Drucker has succinctly described the fundamental shift brought about by the last 10 to 15 years of technology revolution:

"The traditional factors of production – land, labour and capital have not disappeared, but they have become secondary. They can be obtained and easily obtained provided there is knowledge. Knowledge is the new means to obtain social and economic results. It is becoming the only meaningful resource"

Knowledge has become power and it is estimated that more than 1.5 trillion dollars (GigaOm) a year is being invested worldwide in developing new information and communication technologies, software and hardware to exploit knowledge as a driving source of innovation and advantage. It is also estimated that in developed countries three-quarters of the workforce can now be categorised as involved in knowledge work or service (forty years ago that would have been about one third).

The implications are far-reaching for the type of work environment and for the skills people need. Digital knowledge capture, sharing and insight become the new order. Traditional tasks become automated, software carries out the routine and commodity functions, workflow process gets managed by digital communications, paper does eventually become peripheral and people become displaced and dispersed as a more virtual world of remote information and know-how take over.

It places a whole new emphasis on "organisation design" and training and how to manage and get the best out of teams. "Knowledge workers" have become the new champions of the workforce and Computer Weekly in one article dubbed them the "new elite". Those who understand the technology, who are technically literate themselves, who know the basics of architecture and programming, who are up-to-speed with latest software and hardware in so far as it relates to their industry, who have an awareness of how the technology environment around them will evolve, whose understanding is intuitive enough that they can make the technology work for them, rather than be subjected to it… these are the sort of people who may well deserve be to be called the "elite" in this decade. Some people grow up with an innate affinity to technology and to IT generally, others will need to be trained in and learn the requisite skills. Whether a salesperson or a marketer, a finance controller or an analyst, corporate careers will need to be built on a thorough understanding of digital technology and how to leverage and harness the knowledge and insight that can be derived from it.

Knowledge work components

Knowledge work is an interaction between:

- Technology
- Information
- Humans
- Organizations

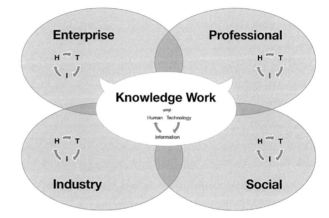

Source: PARC, Mark Bernstein

Xerox embarked on a knowledge project to capture the know-how and expertise of their 25,000 strong service technician workforce that was based all over the world. They realised there was so much knowledge and know-how that was left with the individual that there was a lot of expertise being lost and huge amount of duplication and time invested in working out answers to the same problem. Extensive documentation was, it was felt, not the answer, as their research showed that most technicians could fix most problems. Instead it was the unexpected and the unpredictable that caused delay and customer, as well as technician, frustration.

Xerox's research centre in Palo Alto, PARC, set about working on a new technology solution, it was based around the idea of establishing a social or "water-cooler" network where the shared gossip and experience could be captured and easily accessed. Through multiple field observations and design testing, PARC scientists developed a knowledge-sharing system that codified technicians' tacit know-how, lessons learned, tips and ideas.

It was recognised that to make this work, the technology environment that was created had to be "90% a social process", that its use would evolve over time, that technicians would need to be trained into both the process, how to use it and how to input to it. "Our aim has been to create an intelligent work space that users can adapt and take from it what would be helpful so it becomes a part of their natural process and interactions. We have tested it in different organisational settings and placed high emphasis on the socio-cultural factors of new technology use and adoption"

6. Global – no boundaries: A recent PWC report has been examining the increasingly global nature of the economy. Their key conclusions are no surprise. The world is "getting smaller", 25% of the global workforce is expected to be based in India and a further 20% in China, the aging population in developed countries means a third of workforce there will be over 50 with the possibility that leadership in technology and innovation shifts to a younger, more entrepreneurial Asian business community, cultural and language barriers will continue to decline as social and community networking becomes further established and entrenched, trade tariffs and other artificial barriers will become harder to maintain and senior business leaders will have to have the confidence and skills to step outside geographic and other boundaries and embrace the "global village"

The biggest challenge as already touched upon is that work can be done anywhere. This does not just mean outside the office at home, but in any country anywhere that has adequate communication connections. And the advent of Cloud computing simply reinforces this trend. In a recent review the Economist described how, just as servers, storage and desktops are becoming a "virtual cloud", so we are moving to a point where the labour element of IT will also start to become virtualised". Combine this with a universal skills vocabulary, a universal business language and lower wage costs and we quickly

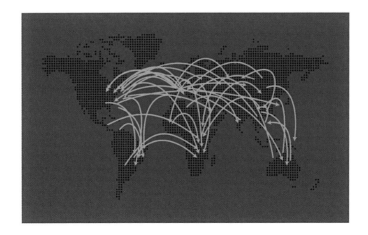

get to a scenario where to keep their jobs the workforce will potentially have to be especially flexible and adaptable, willing to learn but also potentially ready to locate to wherever the knowledge centres of excellence are based.

Of course the "exodus" of jobs from west to east, the brain drain, the growing power of Asian economies, the lower wage rates, the entrepreneurial spirit which is already strong in the developing economies and BRIC in particular has been well-documented and Armageddon scenarios have been variously touted and rehearsed predicting massive unemployment and declining economic prospects among western countries. But those scenarios have been around for some time and we are still yet to see any substantial impact other than slow and incremental change while in fact the major global innovators are still being born out of the west coast of the US, just as they have been for the past 30 years.

What has shifted fundamentally is the mindset required to operate effectively. It has to be global and strategies which are only local in scope are potentially missing big opportunities. That is going to be a key part of the competitive landscape through till 2020 – envisaging and identifying how to scale a new initiative quickly across the world while it is fresh and innovative and different and before it's copied and reengineered by countless others. The new entrepreneurs of the day are coming to market with this way of thinking. The world of boundaries and borders just does not exist. If we can quickly and easily participate in a virtual game with someone in China then why can't we just as easily do business together as well?

7. Automation: Is automation a job killer or a job creator? The international market for automation-related products is estimated at c. Euro300 billion according to Forbes and growth is estimated at 6 to 10% per annum. In Germany, for example, that translates into a Euro 35 billion market place. And, most importantly, it employs some 230,000 people. It has become a major contributor to Germany's electronics industry. It has become so wide-spread that it actually reinforces the attractiveness of Germany as a top industrial location encouraging new companies to set up both domestically and from overseas and all establishing new jobs. Inevitably the skill requirements for these companies require a good to high degree of technology literacy but every organisation requires people at all levels to make things happen. In fact so important is this industry as a job creator that it attracts high level political and state support.

However technology-based industries do not typically promise the same number of local jobs as asset-based production or retail businesses would have. Compare Google with McDonalds: McDonalds employs some 400,000 people worldwide, revenue per average worker of c. $60,000. Google however employs around 25,000 people at average revenue of c. $1m each. The question asked is: what if McDonalds were to become more like Google because of the level of production automation it was able to introduce? Would it keep the same number of employees but shift the work focus to other areas of value add and customer service? Or would it simply reduce the number of people on its payroll?

A 2020 Gartner study considered that the worst case scenario would be characterised by substantial broad-based structural unemployment as machines do more and more of the work that was previously done by people. To avoid such a situation, the Gartner research highlighted that the need for flexibility and adaptability among the workforce would be the key. Moving to where the work is, being ready to reskill and learn new methods and applications, working to contract rather than a job for life, part-time instead of full time, working remotely and not in an office, working for small independent companies rather than big institutions as the smaller organisation takes advantage of the cloud to harness numerous remote supporting technologies and partnerships, self-improvement to continue to learn and develop… all these things will become part of the 2020 work scene. And with it our schools and universities will urgently need to adapt their courses to have an increasing vocational and pragmatic rather than academic output.

★★★★★

Let's leave the final word on the changing 2020 workplace to Philip Tidd, a partner at DEGW, the global strategy consultancy: "What we do know is that in 2020 work will have left the building. Synchronicity and co-location are being turned on their head by new generations and new technology. People will no longer need to be in the same place at the same time every day. We will not need an office, we will connect virtually, the type of work we do will change and the way we interact and depend upon computers will experience a step change too. What we do know is that this will happen. What we don't know is how quickly it will happen or what all the consequences are"

Chapter 9

Omni vs. Multi-Channel: the new organisation paradigm

We are now seeing the rise of "omni-channel". This new phrase has emerged and is being touted as "the next big trend". Apparently it's something different to "multi-channel", which was last year's hot topic. But is there a difference really? Aren't we all in effect saying the same thing? Simply that in this fast-changing world where digital technology is displacing traditional ways of retailing, that to be successful, a retail group needs to operate effectively across all channels, whether it's store, online, mobile, TV or whichever medium the customer is interested in buying. And surely we all get that nowadays, don't we? We've seen the stats, we've experienced the sea-change in consumer habits and preferences, we know surely that to be successful that this is the new game in town and one we need to learn to play.

And while all that's right, it's worth just stopping and reflecting on why this new term "omni" has arisen, why are we being confronted with yet new concepts and challenges, as if the day job isn't demanding enough already!

The answer is because for many, "multi-channel" has actually meant not much more than just the e-commerce /online route to market. Companies have hired "multi-channel" directors where their remit is very simply to head up that new channel, e-commerce, and drive sales online. Their task is to build the digital flagship", to develop engagement with customers in that arena specifically. If there is any "multi-channel" responsibility it's often just about making sure that eg the web site address is on the shopping bag, or the TV ad refers to the web site or that there is a store locator function on the web homepage. Multi has typically meant a focus online with maybe a measure of marketing connectivity that offers some apparent cross-platform communication to customers.

But of course the cross-platform opportunity is bigger than that. And this is where it starts to become difficult. There is the bigger opportunity to provide a unified customer experience. And that means that whatever channel the customer touches they will see the same stock at the same price with the same promotions merchandised in the same way and that connection is made and updated in real time.

That is not easy to do. And that is why for many companies, "multi-channel" has stopped at simple connected marketing. And why most companies have not yet got to that broader "omni" capability. But that omni-capability is worth so much more, that ability to truly engage with customers no matter what the channel and yet provide a seamless and integrated and updated experience.

Let's look at a case study. Aurora Fashions is perhaps an unlikely but certainly excellent example of a retail group who have gone beyond "multi" and embraced "omni". It's been a challenging journey which has taken time and commitment as well as establishing a far-reaching vision of the benefits and business gain to be had.

Aurora Fashions case study

Some years ago, they embarked on their multi-channel journey. Their mission was to be able to do business with their customers "Anywhere and Everywhere". To challenge themselves and to differentiate their mission from the general multichannel talk, they set their sights on delivering the "Omni-channel" experience.

Aurora runs 4 key retail chains. They are Oasis, Coast, Warehouse and Karen Millen. Their IT Director who kick-started this initiative was John Bovill. He was an early advocate and believed that, get this right, and it would not be about cannibalising existing store sales, but quite the contrary, it would be a net driver of sales growth and competitive advantage.

While the early phases of John's journey were to establish the basic functioning of the key transaction web sites, it quickly became clear that as online sales grew so that success also created a problem. How could an online consumer tell if an item was actually in-stock, what if they bought the item online but then the fulfilment team found that the item had been sold, how could Aurora in effect provide some kind-of real time inventory system that would automatically update and so show only what's available, and could they also provide this same system in-store so shop assistants in Southampton could find an item in a store in Aberdeen, and could all this be done in an accurate, up-to-the-minute way so that stores, shoppers and Aurora warehousing and distribution staff could all react immediately and efficiently. And if all that was done, could it be implemented and deployed in such a way that it would in fact drive incremental sales and provide that better and unified customer experience?

Aurora set about that task and it required a major systems alignment and transformation. They appointed Ish Patel as their "Omni-channel director" to coordinate and lead this real –time multi-channel upgrade, they committed significant time and energy to explaining and training so that staff throughout the group would understand and most importantly be able to use the system solution in the way it was envisaged.

And this has now been achieved. Digital commerce has been merged with physical retailing to create a seamless experience for the customer. It has established a new model for stock management as it opens up the whole stock inventory across the full store portfolio. "With our Anywhere Everywhere model, we are saying to customers that if we have it in the UK, then we will get it to you wherever you want it". This is not just true for shoppers online but also for every store. "Every store now has the opportunity to boost sales by fulfilling web orders. It also enables even the smallest store to have access to the Brand's full product range, even to the limited editions".

Stock records are updated in real time. The old approach of updating every 24 hrs is now seen as "dinosaur territory". There is now "seamless integration" throughout the supply chain from Merchandising, Warehousing, Store, Sales analytics, Planning, Customer Services, and Fulfilment. What's more to really drive through the benefits of this, Aurora promise to their customers that they will deliver stock from the store within 90 minutes if the consumer lives in the same town as the stock item is found.

This has led to a 28% uplift in availability of online products and has begun to materially drive extra sales. Online conversion rates doubled. The early metrics showed 10 to 15% uplift in like-for like sales. What's more and what was not expected is that the system enables Aurora to maximise its full price sales. "In some instances full price sales have risen by 80% to 98%. We find we can use this system to highlight product availability and make sure that demand is met and not disappointed. We can be sure therefore to fulfil and every product line gets maximum exposure because it's available "everywhere!"

Store staff have become real enthusiasts as they get credit for the additional sales they can generate through their finding stock for their customers or for assisting in the follow-up local deliveries. Now moving forward, fixed tills are being replaced by iPads which shop assistants carry around with them, "It's more fun, it's much more exciting, it gives us a lot bigger role". Ish Patel (who now leads multi-channel for Victoria's Secrets) commented at the time how this "single view of stock" is very much underpinning how the way Aurora moves forward. And it has become a hallmark also supporting the company's international expansion.

Aurora has been a pioneer, but others are fast catching-up. House of Fraser, Debenhams, Tesco, John Lewis are all vanguard organisations pushing out this omni-channel capability.

Marks and Spencer is said to be investing > £500m in its multi-channel "foundation programme" to also create this single view of stock no matter what the channel in real time. For sure it's not an easy thing to deliver but as others follow Aurora's lead it is clear that "omni-channel" is going to be the way of commerce in the future.

What does this mean for retail and other groups as they start to build their own omni-channel group? What sort of people and skills should they be searching for? Aurora has approached this from an IT /Technical perspective aligning internal systems to present this single view of stock to the customer. And that is without doubt one critical dimension. It's also important that the Marketing Chief is able to match this and in parallel ensure that this integrated internal view is captured and communicated in the most powerful and effective way to the consumer. And with that in mind the marketing team needs to adopt the sort of profile described in a recent job description and candidate search that Digital-360 was involved in.

The multi-channel Marketing Director: Job description

The Marketing Director needs to have a truly Multi-channel outlook and perspective. They must be "the voice of the customer" no matter which way the customer connects with us. This person is the overall champion of the customer experience and has responsibility for ensuring that experience is fully integrated. This means in practice that whether a customer interacts in-store, by phone or online they will see, hear and feel the same thing. All marketing communication needs to be "joined-up" and planned to be complementary and supportive and timely. The customer needs to be comfortable and confident in whatever way they choose to browse or buy. The customer must see the same stock, the same availability, be empowered to eg "phone and reserve" or "click and collect", the pricing and merchandising and special offers must be aligned and the same, they must be able to see their account history no matter which way they have purchased in the past and the Company must be able to recognise and deliver that.

This role is an important step in the Company's journey to deliver a fully integrated, joined-up customer experience. The multi-channel Marketing director must be the champion of this journey. Success will be delivered by reference to specific customer satisfaction scores, increased transaction size and specifically targeted revenue increases.

Retail Week's conferences typically feature a number of speeches and agenda items on this multi vs. omni theme and it's clearly something that retailers want to explore and find out more. But the key message is that omni is useful as a concept to show there is further to go than just the multi solution and that true joined up and integrated customer engagement is yet a step further on this digital journey. For sure it is more challenging and will require more far-reaching change but it is a path that others have shown is possible and it is a path that can produce significant benefits. Without doubt, the winning organisations of tomorrow will be those who have really embraced what this omni-channel world now demands!

Chapter 10:

The 3 Pillars for organisation design

Get 'em, convert 'em, get 'em back!

How should we organise our e-commerce team? Sales are growing, visits to the web site are up, we're recently launched mobile apps, we've got Facebook pages and Twitter feeds and we've got a reasonable-sized team, but how can we take things to the next level of sales growth and profitability? Can we define what are the key skills we should be employing, what are the right interfaces with the rest of the business, should we outsource more, or less, should we have our own technical platform, what do we need to do to be sure we've got the right structures and resources in place to make our e-commerce operation one of the best, and if we continue to invest in this area what kind of ROI should we expecting?

Most companies now have established online businesses and in today's challenging economic climate many are finding that online has become the key source of growth. It is not only generating sales in its own right, and often significant levels of business, but where it is effectively integrated, it is also acting as a strong multi-channel sales tool driving footfall to stores or leads to the call centre, whether through explicit methods like "ring 'n reserve" or "live call back" or by providing a helpful, easy online experience with a clear call to action.

With all this development taking place, it is becoming ever more critical to get the online environment to really work to its best. The potential is clearly there but the challenge now is to truly optimise it, to make sure that the right people are in the right roles doing the right things!

So what is best practice in terms of skills and capabilities? What should this "right team" look like? What are the core jobs and what should those people be focussing on and delivering?

Research is showing that to build a truly effective and powerful e-commerce team, it needs to have 3 core roles at its heart. These 3 roles are the main pillars that will support the whole customer engagement effort and around which the rest of the organisation can be established.

These 3 would report into the Head of e-Commerce and would be key members of the leadership team. They represent the core steps in the value chain, put simply: *get customers, get them to buy, get them to come back!*

- Head of Customer Acquisition
- Head of Customer Conversion
- Head of Customer Retention

Each of these three should be the 3 key hires for any e-commerce organisation. No matter what decisions are made about outsourcing and working with vendors and partners, there needs to be this kind of dedicated focus and skill in-house to take ownership and drive for results. In small or start-up situations, these 3 people would be responsible for a wide range of activities and initiatives and would need to have the experience to prioritise hard as to where best to allocate time and resource. As the business builds so these 3 would naturally bring in expert managers and juniors who would report to them and take on more specific areas of activity.

We can consider in this brief note the following points:

(i)   What is each of the 3 specifically responsible for?
(ii)   What are their core metrics /deliverables?
(iii)   What are the key skills /experience they need to have?
(iv)   What are the other core functions that need to be part of the e-commerce team?
(v)   What overall management team is required?
(vi)   What size should the team be in total?
(vii)   What's the key to making the right level of investment in skills and people?
(viii) A short case study /example

First then, what is each of these 3 responsible for?

- **Head of Customer Acquisition:**

- Paid Search
- SEO
- Affiliates
- Online marketing (which could include campaigns, advertising, email)
- Social media (content development, content distribution and PR)

- Mobile apps development

Key deliverables/metrics:
- *# of visitors*
- *cost /visit*

- **Head of Customer Conversion:**

- User experience
- Market and customer insight
- IA (information architecture)
- site analytics
- design + layout
- functionality, user tools, recommendations etc

Key deliverables/metrics:
- *% conversion visitors to sales*
- *average basket /order size £*

- **Head of Customer Retention:**

- database development
- Email marketing
- CRM (contact strategy, contact programme, loyalty incentives, loyalty partners)

Key deliverables /metrics:
- *% repeat visitors*
- *% repeat purchasers*

(iii) These 3 function /team heads need to have the following skills and experiences:

(i) Significant experience in e-commerce: at least 3 years working in an online transaction environment
(ii) Broad expertise in the specific core area: so for example the Head of Customer Acquisition must have experience not just in Search but across some /all of the other main elements too

(iii) Digital know-how: have knowledge /ideally expertise in all digital channels so online, mobile and also interactive TV (expected to develop further in the next few years)

(iv) Multi-channel savvy: in many companies, digital channels need to work alongside the Store or Call Centre Operations team to drive complimentary activity and customer engagement

(v) Entrepreneurial mind-set: e-commerce generally is still in a high growth phase, it is changing fast, there is need for constant innovation and improvement, structures and processes are not mature, there's plenty of market share to go for! So these people need to have that self-starting hunger and desire, they will need to be able to set their own agenda, they will need to have the determination to constantly improve the customer experience.

(iv). For an e-commerce team to be complete, there are 3 other functions that need to be managed and led. In a Retail market, these are:

- Buying and Merchandising
- Technology
- Fulfilment

These are treated separately because (i) all retailers will often have teams in these areas which can, at least initially, take on the additional e-commerce sales channels as well, and (ii) Technology and Fulfilment for an e-commerce operation can be outsourced. In such circumstances there might need to be an Operations Head on the team in-house who can oversee and manage the outsourcing suppliers but it does potentially remove the need to build and own larger teams.

In Technology, there are a growing number of increasingly sophisticated "white label" outsourced platform providers who can provide the e-commerce backbone. Companies like Venda, who work with TK Maxx, Orange, Wickes, Monsoon, Superdrug and others. Or eCommera, who work with the likes of House of Fraser, Asda, Hamleys and Space.NK. These and other organisations like them have scalable and flexible solutions that enable companies to essentially pay as they go and avoid the substantial risk and cost of building their own.

In Fulfilment, there are out-sourcing companies which range from Royal Mail and UPS to dedicated e-commerce providers like iForce who work with major supermarket chains like Waitrose and Sainsbury's, GSI who work with

Ralph Lauren, Timberland and Dockers and 3P Logistics who fulfil for the likes of Morrisons and the Fashion Hut.

(v). In summary, an e-commerce leadership team might naturally look like this:

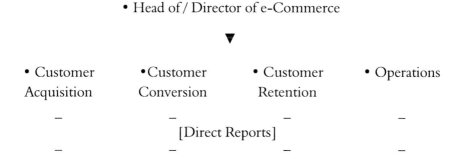

As mentioned, depending on the outsourcing strategy Operations may be split between a Technology Head and a Fulfillment Head. And depending on the size and scale of the business, there might be a separate online Merchandising team.

(vi) Size of team will naturally be driven by the amount of revenue and profit being generated. But there is some investment and risk required at various stages, especially while the business is in its early phases. Many e-commerce operators, especially in today's economic climate, are cautious and would prefer to invest and build behind the revenue, let the business cash flow enable it and then we'll put in the extra resource.

But this is a high growth fast-changing more entrepreneurial environment, and many businesses remain stuck at a certain level unable to really break-through to the next stage of sales growth they aspire to. Often it is not the consumer proposition which is out of sync but simply there isn't the right and sufficient dedicated skills and resources in place to drive this and make this change.

That is why this note talks about the 3 core pillars. Without these 3 people a business will never fulfil its potential; it will never make the break-throughs necessary to get to that next level of customer engagement and experience.

(vii) Where there is hesitation, where there is uncertainty about investment in people and resources, then there is one key that can unlock the potential. That is analytics:

Today, there is a superb array of web analytic tools, many available for free, which will give tremendous insight into the potential of the business.

Many e-commerce businesses get lots of visitors but simply do not convert them into customers. Thousands of people may see the site but only a handful may buy. And many more will never come back. Basic analysis will show why these visitors do not buy. It will show what they do when they arrive, what they look at and at what point they leave. It will show the number of "unfinished check-outs", the number of uncompleted registrations, the % who never progress beyond the first page. It will show where they come from and what sources are driving traffic, and which are not. It can give demographic insight, whether people enjoy and would recommend the site and show the strength of positive and negative sentiment toward the overall online experience

What analysis can also show is what's missing, what revenues could be generated if the problem areas were addressed, if the conversion ratio was closer to best practice, if the customer experience was optimised. That will show the potential ROI; the return a business can get if it has the people and resource to go after these problem areas and turn them into practicable and realisable opportunities. That can be the key, the catalyst. That can help persuade a board of investors to take that next step, bring in the right people, staff up the 3 Pillars, because the size of the prize can be quantified and measured and the return can be captured.

(viii) Successful e-commerce businesses today are typically fanatical about analysis and the numbers. Companies like Asos.com, AO.com, eBay, Amazon.com and many others.

They pour over the key trends and metrics, they analyse site performance, they are constantly identifying new ways to optimise performance, to tweak up the sales conversion ratio, to push up average basket size, to increase the % of repeat purchases. The analytics can clearly demonstrate that if they make a change here its impact on sales can be quantified. It gives them and the investors the confidence to bring in new people, to get that dedicated eg user experience expert, to staff up the "3 Pillars", to target and go after the ROI, to provide the skills and the resources to capture that latent value and help build and drive the business to the next stage.

Chapter 11:

Building a successful e-commerce business: how to establish the "virtuous cycle" of sustainable self-funding growth and development

Here is a common story I hear: "everyone speaks about the opportunity in digital and e-commerce, and I'm sure we could build out successful new revenue streams. But it all comes down to investment, and often requests for substantial investment. Each business has plans to hire people, build tech platforms, add to marketing costs yet it's all based on guesstimates and forecasts and they may be too optimistic. Is there another way to develop this area while managing the up-front costs and investment risk"?

The answer is that there is another way and one which is potentially a lot easier. And it is *self-funding*. It simply provides a sustainable way to maximise the growth in the e-commerce operation. And in doing so generate additional streams of revenue, and profit, that can be used to justify continued investment.

This alternative approach is the "Virtuous Cycle of e-Commerce investment". It consists of just three keys. And it's all about having the right people in place. The business needs just 3 key people: a Head of Conversion, a Manager of Analytics and a Web Master. These 3 work "hand-in-glove" to create a virtuous cycle of activity.

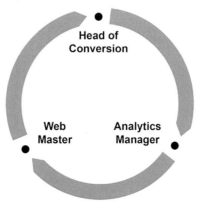

1. The Head of Conversion

This person is responsible for converting traffic to sales. They are not involved in acquiring traffic. They are not a Search /PPC /Affiliates expert. They are however insiders, looking at what happens at the next stage of the value chain. Once we've got the traffic what are we doing with them?

Their key remit is looking at the web site /user experience. They are the ones who are constantly examining the site information architecture, the layout of the content, the look and feel of the web site, the whole end-to-end user experience. What happens to people once they arrive>? What parts of the online store do they visit? And what parts never seem to get many visitors. How long do people stay? What engages them and what puts them off? How many put items in a basket, and how many never complete that basket, what if we change this instruction or make this process shorter or skip this section or put this button in highlights, does any of that make a difference?

At the end of the day this is in many ways the key role in an e-commerce organisation, and it needs someone dedicated to this task. Someone who has only one very clear metric and focus in mind. What is the % conversion ratio? And yes, there are subsidiary ratios such as average basket size and ave. number of items ordered. But visits: sales is the key.

And yet most e-commerce operations do *not* have one of these people. This key role is often subsumed within a broader role of Online Marketing Manager or Web Site Manager. And as a result the focus is often lost. And often, not surprisingly visits: sales ratios are not as leveraged as they could /should be.

2. Analytics Manager

This person is one of the two key partners to our Head of Conversion. This person is in charge of all the data. They have been tasked to ensure that there is a proper and effective web analytics process and data-gathering capability in place. And their task is to provide the analysis and insight that can show what improvements can be made.

They have the opportunity to provide the *weekly change agenda*. They should be in a position to know where each visitor goes and where they fall away. There is the classic waterfall analysis that shows for each 100 visitors how many make it all the way though to check-out and purchase? How many does the site lose even at the home page? How many get to the registration page for example and drop out there? How many baskets are set-up and left uncompleted?

And if these Analytics Managers are in any way curious they will be not just the analysers of the data.. But they will be the interrogators too! They will want to understand why it is that people drop out or don't complete? They will want to be holding regular focus groups and pieces of research to ask visitors: what went wrong, why did you not complete, and most importantly what could we have done differently that would have made your experience easier, better, more enjoyable, more convenient, simpler, more compelling so that you would have completed?

And they would also be constantly reviewing best practices and asking why can't we match them? So everyone knows and talks about Amazon's One Click ordering process for example. But how many companies offer that facility aside from Amazon? Here we are some years on from when that simple but powerful piece of functionality was first introduced. But how few today copy or offer that? But the technology to do is now straightforward as many web site platforms do offer the facility to save credit card details for future ordering. But where is the One Click button?

3. The Web Master

So we have the Conversion head who is orchestrating and driving to generate higher sales from the marketing and online activity. We have the analytics and insight that shows what can be improved and where the key opportunities lie. Now all we need is the final piece of the jigsaw>

And this is the Web Master. This person is the one who implements the technical changes that have been identified. It's about working closely with the Conversion Manager to identify the highest priorities for change, the items that will make the biggest differences to sales.

They then have the technical capability and importantly, the access, to make those changes to the site. Oftentimes this may be simple changes to content or moving layout or information or making some things more prominent or reducing the number of pre-registration questions or adding in a piece of functionality. Each item may in itself be quite small but its impact can be quite high. Many are the stories of eg moving a Next Step button above the fold and seeing basket completion jump by 20%.

But what is key here, is that this Web Master has access. This person needs to have the agility to get to the source code and the authority to change things.

What this needs to avoid, and it's situation which is very common today, where the e-commerce team want to make changes requiring technical input and then they get told that they will have to wait for IT team resource, that there is a queue of projects from across the whole company waiting to be implemented, that this e-commerce initiative will have to wait till resource can be allocated and found. And oh, by the way, that will be in 6 month's time.

What this Web Master also needs is the skill to think and act quickly and entrepreneurially. What shortcut might exist that could enable this change to be made easily? Is there already a piece of eg Open Source software ready developed that could perhaps be adapted and deployed. Is there some solution in the Cloud that might enable this problem to be outsourced or solved in a different way?

What is key is that the tasks and changes need to be done quickly. They cannot sit in a 6 month queue. E-Commerce as indeed all technology today does not sit in traditional legacy system lead times. Things are moving at such a apace that they need to be captured now!

Implications and Conclusion

Achieving this virtuous cycle is not hard. It's mostly about formalising and focusing current resources onto these key priorities. Such people also need not be high cost and often young rising stars with a few years good online and e-commerce experience should be able to adapt and respond to the challenge.

The main process change is enabling a Web Master to have access and authority. That may require the approval of the Senior IT Director and may require some initial partnering and working with the IT team to ensure good governance and safe management. But again it should not be difficult to achieve.

What is clear is that the best e-commerce sites are achieving very high growth rates, they are hitting that virtuous cycle where not only can they make changes quickly internally but their success reaches out and creates that buzz and excitement that makes a difference, that gets people talking about the business, that encourages more visitors and gets more recommendations from friends, family and supporters.

And here's a brief case study to finish: www.zulily.com is a highly successful clothing /apparel e-commerce business selling beautiful and competitively-priced clothing for young children, from about 6 months old to about age 8. It only set up about 3 yrs ago but has quickly established itself as a leading online kids clothing store in the US. And it launched in UK start of 2012 as part of a potential broader global expansion.

Why so successful so quickly? (sales have topped >$700m). While it has for sure been innovative in its merchandising and consumer offers, a key element of their whole approach has been to put a heavy reliance on analytics. There is an Analytics team who are monitoring site performance 24 /7/365. They are looking all the time, in real time, what is working and what is not, what items are selling, what is attracting consumer interest, what is stimulating to purchase? And they are working closely with their Conversion team and Web Master group to evaluate the data, draw out the key conclusions, identify the priorities *and make those changes*, now!

There is no delay. The analysis does not wait for eg the weekly trading meeting. It does not wait for an IT team to decide when and if it will make changes. The whole visit to sale conversion experience is being constantly and continuously optimised. And in this way Zulily are ensuring that the visitor experience is enjoyable and easy, that customer satisfaction is at its highest, that problems are identified and resolved immediately, that sales and revenues are maximised!

Chapter 12

Case study: e-Commerce team structure for ABC Company

This is a case study illustration and sets out a possible e-Commerce team structure for example company ABC.

In practice, this particular company is a market-leading organisation. It has had a basic web site and online presence for some years. It has now decided to really drive out its digital capabilities and customer engagement. It also has concluded that it does have a significant e-commerce opportunity and potential revenue upside.

The structure and team skills discussed then in this chapter are especially relevant for a company looking to move up its digital activities to the next stage of customer impact.

At ABC, the existing Marketing and IT team wish to define future digital team shape and objectives for the next wave of growth and development. Their plans and roadmap are set out here in case study format.

1. Vision//structure/goals/roadblocks

(i) Vision:

- to build online revenues to £50m by end 2017

(ii) Structure:

For Now:

- to develop the e-commerce team into a measurably effective unit with clear KPi which can be monitored to show milestone progress and revenue development

- to place greater emphasis on the key stages of the e-commerce value chain and to appoint managers to take responsibility for each of those key stages
- to be evolutionary and embrace the skills and expertise which already exists within the e-commerce team today
- to be supportive of the people and respect their individual worth and contributions

By 2017:

To move over time to implement a multi-channel strategy which can deliver a fully integrated customer experience. The aim is that the company markets and presents itself with one voice, one coherent and consistent product and marketing presentation and champions and enables customers to interact in store, online or by phone with ease.

(iii) Key goals:

- drive revenue to £8m this year and target £50m by 2017
- build an online presence which people talk about with passion and enthusiasm and are proud to recommend to friends and colleagues
- work with IT to provide a seamless, easy, scalable and highly functional e-comm technology platform
- ability to respond in real time to customer needs
  develop effective cross-functional support with other departments

(iv) Key constraints/roadblocks today in the company:

- Site IT does not work well today (eg site performs slowly /products disappear!)
- The platform is being relaunched but meantime there are long delays in any interim tactical improvement plans and lack of appropriately skilled IT resources.
- Target salary levels for key individuals in the e-Commerce team are currently budgeted bottom quartile
- This impacts quality of hire and levels of skills of people who do join to be able to hit the ground running, they need to be trained up which delays their impact and contribution.
- A lack of understanding generally across the business about the breadth and complexity of building a successful e-commerce business, about the different

skills required starting with: customer acquisition, IT site build, user optimisation, online branding /marketing, content/ editorial, online merchandising and IA, transaction and payment management, sales conversion, customer service, CRM and then through to fulfilment and returns.

- A prioritisation of work across different departments which can often mean significant delays or lack of attention to the Online business.

In any discussion on team and skills, it is worth emphasising that organisation structures need to be fluid and evolving. One of the key drivers will be to work around the skills and expertise of the people already in the organisation. Another will be the continuing fast pace of change in the e-commerce world which is identifying new skill /new value-added areas which may need to be embraced and incorporated.

2. Proposed team structure

This proposed team structure is designed to drive the next stage of e-commerce revenue growth. And it is set against the backcloth of the constraints and roadblocks described above.

Specific structure goals:

There will be 5 key reports to the Head of e-Commerce:

i.   **Customer Acquisition Manager**
ii. **Customer Conversion Manager**
iii. **(Customer Retention Manager**
iv. **Content / Category Manager**
v.   **Programme / Ops Manager**

(2) (i) The Customer Acquisition Manager

(get 'em to visit! / footfall)

Key responsibilities:

- responsible for all the key ways to drive potential customers to the online buying experience.

- will include Paid Search (PPC), Search Engine Optimisation (SEO),
- will also include the establishment of key traffic-driving partnerships online as well as broader opportunities.
- consideration of selected Affiliates
- social media engagement
- advertising both online and offline eg drive to store and web site print campaign to create awareness /promote key seasonal merchandise and multi-channel customer opportunity

Who reports in:

- online marketing exec (general marketing)
- online marketing exec (online partnerships)
- Search PPC/ SEO person
- Social Media? (currently sits in Marketing)

Success metrics for this role:

- # unique visitors
- # uniques by source eg number from partnerships /number from Search /number from Social Media
- cost of paid search /customer acquired
- click through rates on advertising
- tracked advertising click-throughs to purchase consideration

(2) (ii) The Customer Conversion Manager

(get 'em to buy)

Key responsibilities:

- responsible for number of visitors who complete and purchase online
- optimising the user experience to continue to improve dwell time on site and bag/ basket completion
- working with Site Analytics to identify what working online and what not
- establishing an ongoing and weekly agenda of site improvements that need to be addressed with clear recommendations as to requirements

- working with Creative Dept. and /or the site Design agency to identify issues that require minor redesigns eg move click button to different part of page
- working with Web Master /IT resource to implement changes
- carry out these tactical Design /IT changes and ensure that job gets done very quickly
- identifying new functional tools that will strengthen customer engagement

Who reports in:

- Site designer
- UX
- Analytics

Success metrics for this role:

- (should show increasing progress and upward trends to at least match best practice benchmarks in the sector)
- % conversion ratio (visitors: sales)
- ave. basket size
- UX positive comment trends
- reduced bounce rate
- reduced checkout uncompleted baskets rate

(2) (iii) The Customer Retention Manager

(get 'em to come back)

Key responsibilities:

- responsible for driving customer lifetime value
- this involves identifying key means to build relationships with existing customers
- and encourage /drive repeat purchase
- will require the establishment /further development of an online customer database with their email addresses
- regularly cleansed to ensure up-to-date

- a programme of outbound marketing to target customers with differentiated communications to reflect eg active vs lapsed, UK vs overseas, hi income vs mid income etc
- development of other tools to encourage repeat purchasing, eg loyalty incentives, privileged invitations etc
- this may also involve social media activity

Who reports in:

- CRM /database
- email marketing

Success metrics for this role:

- # of repeat purchasers
- size of eg "loyalty club"
- ave. basket size of repeat purchasers
- customer life time value of this group eg top 1000 by estimated value.

(2) (iv) The Content / Category Manager

(get 'em engaged)

Key responsibilities

- responsible for the Product /Copy /Editorial and Photographic content on the site
- a major role in charge of the way the site looks and feels
- quality of photography and image resolution
- the copy descriptions
- signage
- overall online merchandising and design lay-out
- Information Architecture to optimise visual presentation
- definition of key product categories
- ensuring each category is easily found by site visitors and provides a compelling experience
- product and information hierarchy

- working with Customer Conversion Manager to identify which products /categories working best and identifying opportunities for improvement
- provision of content /copy for distribution by Marketing to social media sites

Who reports in:

- Product /Category execs
- Visual Merchandising
- Editorial copy editor
- editorial /copy exec
- Studio team :photography + styling

Success metrics for this role:
- % customers surveyed rating site look and feel
- positive sentiment trends through social media comment
- timely upload of new photography and product detail
- % visitors moving from product to checkout pages
- 0 site glitches /bugs in terms of product presentation /product availability
- key social media site # of interactions /positive comments to distributed copy /content

(2) (v) The Programme / Ops Manager

(make it happen!)

Key responsibilities:

- responsible for the delivery of the key major change programs for the e-Commerce team
- specific charge to deliver the new site relaunch.
- extensive and ongoing interface with IT and with the key technology partner as well as coordinating with other key departments eg Marketing to ensure appropriate levels of support and publicity
- site pre-launch testing and QA
- this role will also be responsible for the key Phase 2 post launch bug fix and site management to ensure the site works as planned

- this person will also take on-going responsibility for site IT liaising with the IT team but dealing with and taking responsibility for tactical IT issues which affect the day-to-day working of the site and liaising with IT resources to ensure issues are resolved immediately
- and the role will have an overall Operations responsibility that extends specifically through to Fulfilment and ensuring that Logistics is managing effectively timely delivery and returns management
- this will likely lead to the setting up of a Fulfilment Steering Cmttee that this person will chair and which will involve input and participation from IT and Logistics

Who reports in:

- Project exec
- Web Master
- + tactical IT web development (to be confirmed)

Key success metrics:

- delivery of site relaunch
- on time in full on budget ("OTIFOB")
- Zero bugs by end of year
- 24/7 real time resolution of site technical issues
- 24/7 real time capability to update /change content and tactical IA
- establishment of Fulfilment Steering Cmttee
- size of returns
- % deliveries completed on time

3. Team gaps

The team structure just described will provide a natural evolution for the existing team. It will also provide a step-up challenge for the existing staff as their roles now become more focussed and there is greater emphasis on KPi/ key deliverables and measures of success.

This approach will provide greater clarity on what is working and contributing to revenue growth and profit development, and which areas are not. So it should enable a stronger drive to ROI.

However, as mentioned, e-Commerce is evolving fast and there are three particular areas which may need to be provided for with specialist skills brought in:

Mobile is more and more critical as a necessary communications channel. And Mobile is a critical way for people to search, browse and buy.

At present, Mobile is an area which ABC is not proactively exploring. It does require specialist skills and know-how. For example the online site needs to be reconfigured so it works and is user-friendly on each of the main Mobile OS and handsets. Key apps should be developed and maintained which allow instant access to rich content, click and reserve and easy buy. Mobile resource(s) could form part of the next stage recruitment plan for the e-Commerce team.

Social Media is an increasing driver of site traffic and an increasing influence on Brand perception. This is another area that will quickly need more specialist attention and resource.

At present it sits within the Marketing department and functions alongside PR. But there is a case to say this function should be more firmly rooted in the e-Commerce group given how much social media activity that is now taking place online and on Mobile and how important it is becoming

Lastly IT: online is of course very closely aligned and dependent upon scalable, Agile, real time /fast response technology that can enable ABC to quickly adapt to changing customer needs and expectations

This does not suggest that IT should now be part of the e-Commerce team. But it does suggest that there should be resource in IT which is dedicated to supporting the e-commerce platform and enabling quick changes to be made.

A Web Master could for example still be a part of the IT team but might need to sit day-to-day with e-Commerce and share responsibility for the ongoing and tactical changes to improve the whole web site experience.

In addition, the current plan in the short term places significant dependence on the IT third party Partner to build, deliver and be available to upgrade the web site on a continuing basis. This places some risk on the business and it's recommended that some IT web development resource be established in-house that can more efficiently manage the third party partnership to control risk and delivery and ensure there is greater capability in the ABC team to take ownership of the online environment and its reliability.

Chapter 13

Impact of Digital on Marketing /Marketing Department organisation structures

1. Background

In the good old days! Marketing was relatively straightforward to organise. Back in the 1970's when the marketing function really began to gain widespread recognition and adoption, there were typically just a few key levers that the department was responsible for. And these were mostly around building brand awareness among the target customer /consumer group.

Today's world however has become infinitely more challenging and complex. The role and responsibility of marketing has grown significantly. Companies today now almost universally look to their marketing team as their engine of growth. Market sectors are more competitive, they are usually global, they have become multi-channel, technology is proving disruptive while at the same time being attractive, expertise eg in mobile, social, SEO is becoming more specialist and harder to obtain… getting any increase in market share and gains in revenue is just more challenging.

The progressive marketing function however is now looking to tackle these challenges head-on. They are taking responsibility for developing the company's strategy and plans that can navigate through this market maze and develop winning solutions. The need for an integrated, multi-channel, technically literate, innovative and ever more entrepreneurial team is now becoming paramount.

This chapter looks at the evolution of the marketing organisation. It starts with "the good old days" and looks at where things now are. There is no "right/proven" structure and model. Every company of course is different. There are differences in B2B and B2C (principally B2B much less sophisticated and developed) and companies are very influenced by number of products /number of Brands, number of countries sold to, size of revenue streams, readiness of the senior directors /officers of the company to invest, how responsive the business is to emerging new channels of communication like web, mobile, social, and just how challenging the marketing team wants to be.

2. The good old days

There were principally two key levers: Promotions and Advertising.

The Proms team developed the annual plan and set out the promotions cycle. They would agree plans with Sales dept. about what sort of incentives required at different stage of the sales cycle. Activity would be driven mostly by the Sales team and the needs of key Trading customers. So there would be something planned for each quarter. The range of options was fairly basic, choose from direct mail, sampling, discounts and if possible eg "on-pack" competitions.

Alongside this and in support would be the *Product /Brand advertising*. This would depend on budgets and would be all about building awareness and recognition. It might be on TV or in Print or on the Radio. (Media buying and planning would invariably be outsourced to the Ad agency)

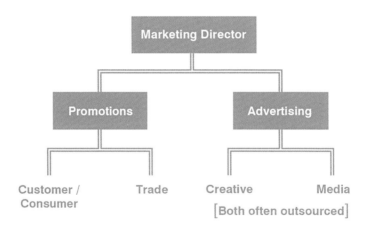

3. The 1990's

Still before the real commercial advent of the internet, yet Marketing even at this point was becoming significantly more sophisticated. The catalyst here was the availability of data and more and more computer processing power available on the desktop. Suddenly a marketing team could recruit in a data /insight /research team who could analyse customer behaviour, spot trends, engage in richer and deeper segmentation and identify much more tailored and refined and sophisticated marketing campaigns and activities.

So marketing teams might typically have a Head of Insight (in early days this might have been the Market Research Mgr), who would take responsibility for data and analytics. The work might be outsourced to a specialist data/research team or combined with some in-house expertise.

In addition, the whole concept of the "Brand" began to take root. Brand Mgrs. began to proliferate as companies looked at the pioneer of effective Brand marketing, Procter & Gamble, and wanted to adopt and copy their, it seemed, proven success model. Brand Mgrs. were charged with being the "guardians of the brand". While no-one was quite sure what that meant! it seemed mostly about measuring and monitoring Brand awareness, propensity to purchase and brand sentiment. It also meant being the champion of the brand internally across the company. That usually also meant being the coordinator of brand planning, brand budgets, brand promotions, brand development and brand advertising. And in some instances having those skills reporting directly into them rather than being separated out.

But this era did particularly herald a step-change in the profile and power of Marketing. Marketing Directors began to appear on the main board. The Brand Mgr started to become a powerful figure of influence and responsibility. The team became more than just administrators of a promotions budget. They became responsible formally with Sales for top line revenue growth, and often took on the Brand/Product P&L. They also had a much more involved role in the long term. No longer just about short term tactical campaigns and quarterly sales programmes. There was now also a key responsibility to use the data and insight to generate product development programmes which would keep the Brand alive and contemporary and compelling.

4. Now!

Today's world has seen a step change in complexity. We now live in this multi-channel, technology-enabled world of innovation, new ideas and constant change. Channels to market have proliferated and fragmented. It's no longer a simple world of TV, Print, Radio. Now add of course so much more whether via mobile, tablet, webcast, YouTube, Pinterest, Facebook, Twitter, social media monitoring generally, in-game advertising, pre-roll, SEO, SEM, blogs, eCRM, e-Commerce… the list goes on.

And yet, this has all fallen to the Marketing Department. No other team has stood up and tried to take this all on board. And typically no other team in the company would naturally have the skills or market understanding to adopt and embrace all this change and opportunity. So everyone now looks to Marketing. Tell us about these changing market/multi-channel/omni-channel conditions, how do we now reach out to our target audience (they are no longer where they used to be!), get us the data and insight that enables us to understand what marketing communications will work and what will not, conduct the tests that show how to engage with our target customers in this digital world, identify the new programmes and activities and product development which will ensure we remain/become successful!

No small challenge.

And so the Marketing department has had to evolve rapidly. It has had to take on and recruit new skills/new people. It has had to expand simply to cover the basics. It now is expected to have skills in all these "new" areas and to understand mobile, social, Twitter etc etc. Over the course of the past decade marketing teams have grown in numbers (though not necessarily in comms spending budgets) and have become even more "centre stage". They are now the champions of not just the Brand, but also of the Customer. They now formulate the total customer engagement strategy. Instead of Sales driving Marketing (as used to happen), it's now the other way round. Marketing are the key. They are the ones who are at the heart of the business. It is their knowledge about digital and the changing market environment that is dictating the whole organisation's future strategy. It is now Marketing's relationship with IT that is the core team dynamic. It is how those two departments operate and collaborate and work effectively together that will ultimately decide who will be the winners by 2020.

So in the next two diagrams/org structures, the first illustration shows how the Marketing skills set has proliferated and the range of new skills and functions the team had to adopt. The second chart next page shows how the better Marketing departments have come to terms with this, how they have reorganised to manage that proliferation to find a new simpler more streamlined more manageable and more effective org.solution.

As mentioned at the beginning of this note, there are no "right answers". And this has simply tried to show how things have changed, and by just how much! And what some possible ways of navigating the organisation through this changing dynamic period might look like.

(i) Extended Marketing value chain /org.:

(ii) a Streamlined /consolidated Marketing organisation structure:

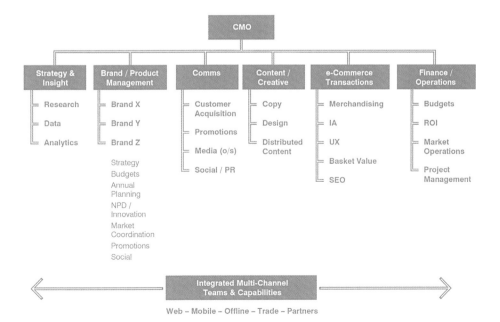

Chapter 14

Multi-national Marketing: impact of digital on organisation structures

Against the global background of digital innovation and transformation, Marketing is facing its own challenges. The move to a multi-channel /omni-channel world is changing the whole marketing mix and requiring investment in new skills, technical literacy and ways of understanding what customers will best respond to. Whether Business or Consumer, expectations are the same: customers are increasingly demanding self-serve value and convenience.

So how for example should a Marketing team organise itself to meet this fast-changing environment? For sure they do need "digital skills", they do need people who really get this "new marketing agenda" and have the know-how, best practices, war stories and lessons learned of what works, and what does not! But Marketing also needs to find ways to integrate these skills and organise so it can embrace them.

The challenge is that most companies of course do not start with a blank sheet of paper. They do have existing system and processes, they have teams who have worked with them often for many years, they may be global in span and operation, they will have other demands and priorities on their time, not all their customers will want digital comms and interaction, not all their teams will know how to start testing out and exploring the digital agenda.

Because of this most companies will often start by appointing eg a "Chief Digital Officer". This is someone who is the champion of all things digital. This is an educator, an informer, a voice of influence, a home of best practice, a driver of change. Often this person will recruit a small team of like-minded digital experts who can spread the net wider. This team too will often take on specific responsibilities, pilot new ideas, establish platforms eg in e-commerce, build key relationships with agencies and third party providers in this space. They will also typically encourage local teams in international markets to establish their own in-house digital capability. This enables the digital team and capability to grow more quickly and builds a network of key local "in-brand" /in-house digital advocates.

At some point this network will grow so that we see the beginnings of a "hub and spoke" model. That is a core digital expert team at the centre continuing to push the digital strategy, testing new opportunities and supplemented by "spokes", key talent in local subsidiary business units who take charge of local digital tactics and implementation. This might especially be around Search marketing, local advertising, local online promotions etc.

Some key questions can be identified which might influence and drive how this "hub and spoke" model might take shape for an organisation: it's a digital marketing structuretest.

Digital Marketing: 6 keys questions to determine how to organise at a multi-national level?

1. What is current infrastructure?
- number of people
- where they are located /number of different locations
- what sort of skills

2. How many Brands with online potential?
- number of brands with multi-country reach
- demand for digital for each /variation by country

3. Current status of each Brand /in each key national market
- has own online site today?
- amount of traffic /visitors?
- the Brand's desire to use online to grow the business?
- e-commerce potential?

4. What's the potential multi-country reach?
- how many brands have a multi-country audience and reach today?
- what's the potential?
- do they all aspire to be global?

5. Current structure
- who is responsible for Online /Digital today?

- any central control or all distributed around the businesses
- who has more control /influence in this area: IT or Marketing or Group

6. What KPI if any exist today around brand marketing effectiveness?
- is culture /control driven from the centre or it dispersed /localised?
- how are brands measuring digital interest and demand?

Developing some understanding of each company's situation can help define the hub and spoke model and determine what key skills and responsibilities should be established where.

It is possible to consider some radical options such as everything digital is outsourced, or everything is centralised in a hub or everything is decentralised into local markets. There is no "right" or "wrong answer", what works for one organisation may not work for another and any solution needs to fit company culture, readiness for change, how demanding for digital are its customers, amount of resource and investment available and how passionate and committed to "digital" are the senior management of the company. But certainly the model that most organisations are working with today is some variation on a hub and spoke model.

Digital organisation options:

(i) In-house vs. Outsource

(ii) All centrally located /controlled:
- "a centre of excellence"
- managing all strategy, planning and administering all local execution
  This avoids duplication of resource and effort and each local market "reinventing the wheel" for itself and perhaps making the same mistakes.

(iii) All distributed to the spokes
This provides stronger local ownership but likely leads to duplication of cost and also of resource, disparate and sometimes confusing presentation of the Brand, no coordinated marketing, different customer experiences which may lead also to disappointment and loss of engagement.

(iv) Hub 'n Spoke

Spoke could include:
- local national Customer Acquisition:
  - Search, both SEO and SEM,
  - local partnerships
  - local affiliates
  - local content and updating
  - local store finder
  - any click n' reserve /click n'collect solutions
- Customer services
- Fulfilment /delivery

Customer Acquisition could start in Hub in initial phases till reach local scale

Hub could include:
- all Technology
  - e-commerce platform
  - Web Master
  - Mobile developments /apps
- all Customer Analytics /Conversion
  - UX
  - design
  - analytics
- all Customer Retention
  - CRM software eg Salesforce.com
  - Data analysis /segmentation /data insight
- Social Media
  - this can be critical to control, monitor and influence in coordinated and consistent way what is said about a global /international brand and to manage its online reputation.

★★★★★

This whole area of how to organise in Marketing to facilitate and enable the most effective marketing to customers is a big topic and this note can only begin to set out some of the challenges and options.

This same set of issues is also very relevant to IT. How Marketing is organised needs to also reflect any developments and change to the company's technology team structures. And if "hub and spoke" is an appropriate framework for the Marketing team then it's likely that the same market and customer drivers should indicate the direction that IT should also be organising around.

Most companies will typically start to address these challenges by establishing a "Digital Steering Committee". This group will be made up of all key stakeholders and likely include the CMO, the CTO and head of key Brands or Business Units. A common solution can be identified that can work at least for the core brands and businesses to start with. What is critical to recognise is that any solution must be regularly reviewed and checked that it is still appropriate. This digital world is of course moving so quickly that what is right for today may not suit the company as it evolves and reaches higher levels of digital maturity.

Chapter 15:

Retail time bomb!

The internet is making retail real estate redundant. It's been suggested that by 2030 there will be no shops at all as people browse, search and buy online!

Online shopping is becoming more and more sophisticated and engaging and convenient and reliable and safe. Products can now be presented beautifully (eg Zulily.com), product information and comparison can be limitless (eg eBay, Coats.com), 3D imagery is growing (eg in R&D at Tesco, new Sony 3D laptops), sound and associated video explanations are now common (eg Screwfix.com), social media allows us to chat and compare while browsing and you can even "co-browse", looking at the same screen (eg United Cloud), we can access the information on-the-go on our mobiles and iPads, we can use location-based tools to find our nearest shop, the best local bargains, check if product in stock, and in just a few years now we will be able to view a holographic display in front of us at our voice command (Augmented Reality projects are already in the lab and just a step away from being commercialised), removing the need and "barrier" of having to hold a screen or machine.

While the 2030 prediction may be an exaggeration, all agree that the online shopping world is where all the growth and fun and excitement and innovation is taking place. More and more people are choosing to shop online and they are doing this in preference to visiting the shops. Sure the family might visit one of the big shopping malls at a weekend as much for a family day out to look, touch, feel, see what's new, look at prices and have lunch. But the actual purchase is often now being made back at home later that day when they can compare prices and get the best deal and bargain. They might use cash back sites like Quidco, Groupon daily deals with friends, private sale /by invitation only discounts such as Achica, or on eBay which has long given up on just cheap second hand goods, or catch any of the large number of brand and designer label end of season /end of range but great value sites from Net-a-Porter and Asos to Brand Alley and MandM.

And in times of economic uncertainty, isn't it just inevitable that with pressure on consumer budgets they will find it more and more attractive to shop in this way?

In which case, why do retailers continue to build more bricks 'n mortar retail estate? The big supermarkets especially have announced big plans in recent times to continue to expand their footprint (more than 25million square feet!) and you only have to pick up the latest copy of Retail Week, the trade mag, to read of yet another retailer looking to grow by expanding the number of shops ("over 50% of 212 European retailers have announced plans recently to add 10 or more stores over next 2 years")

Why? Why build when basic retail economics show that it will only take a small shift in the amount bought in the stores to switch to online and it is just no longer viable to continue to keep the shop open? Analysis shows that on average it only takes a 15% decrease in sales to push a store into loss.

Right now, shop closures are being blamed on the tight economy and tight budgets. The implications are that when the economy booms all these shops will now experience a resurgence of shopper visits and spending and all suddenly recover their revenues and profitability. But what is not being said so plainly is that just may not ever happen! What we have seen over the past decade is a true paradigm shift in consumer behaviour. There is now a new way to shop and consume. People don't need so many shops. And when they do shop their needs are becoming different. They want the showcase destination experience where they can view the biggest and widest and most exciting range and opportunity. They don't want for sure small secondary high streets where availability is limited and the shopping experience is boring.

It's been said that typically in the UK the average chain will need no more than 30 shops. That will cover all the major conurbations. And such a size and concentration has more chance of economic viability than chains of 80 or 100 plus shops spread all over.

Moving to this new style and size of retail portfolio is made even more urgent when considering recent research from Deloitte. They calculate that if all the virtual selling space that has been added by retailers over the past 10 years is added up and "converted" into the equivalent of bricks n' mortar retail selling space then that's a further 56 million square feet of property. That's a lot of space! No surprise then that online is making so much existing physical retail space redundant.

Few would now argue that we are now entering a new era of retail landscape where retailers will have to take a much more aggressive multi-channel approach and make their stores work with their online environment and use one to drive footfall and visits to the other all to encourage purchasing, no matter where the final transaction takes place. Initiatives which for many are still a major innovation but which will be critical are Click and Collect, or Ring and Reserve, or Visit Reserve and Buy when you get home. Whatever the combination, this future is something retailers must grapple with and evolve their business models and organisation structures to cope with and use it to drive sustainable profit growth.

Meantime the retail time bomb is ticking. All retailers are affected. It's no longer just about CDs and DVDs, and soon likely may be no bricks 'n mortar opportunity left to purchase such items. It's also not just electricals like Comet, Jessops and Dixons as they struggle to survive. It's about all sectors, and clothing specially now is finding substantial pressure from the online world (from Very to BooHoo and even Oxfam!)

Change is a must but still today few retailers have evolved and grasped the nettle. Yes they have their web site, yes you can buy online (though often the user experience is poor) but many have cut back on investment as they face the need to really upgrade their back-end technology to cope with and meet growing consumer demand and desire for a really good browsing and buying experience. Property companies with a focus for retailer commercial development are another related group under pressure. They will soon find that unless they have most of their investment in large malls then their secondary high street portfolio will rapidly become valueless.

The need for change is staring them in the face, Digital technology is creating a whole new world of opportunity and ability to engage with customers in the way they want and give them the multi-channel experience they crave. It does require investment, it does require change, it may need new systems, it may need new processes and ways of working, it may mean abandoning decades old ways of working (eg no longer need that big Property department). It needs transition planning and management and longer term horizons. Who is going to stand up and be counted, who will be in the vanguard? The likes of Tesco often get quoted for what they are achieving. The Argos business model is so geared up for this new world that they should be everyone's favourite. But M&S is only now in 2013 starting to build their own e-commerce platform (been relying on Amazon for all that) and Morrisons is only now just tentatively beginning to build a capability to shop online and the emphasis there is non-core non-food. "Traditional" retailers have been slow to change and that's why there's so much going on with the new ventures like ChemistDirect, BrandAlley and AO.com who can capture today's consumer need quickly. How many of our current "retail champions" are going to survive this era of digital transformation and still be leaders in 2020?

Chapter 16

e-Commerce international expansion in Europe: the immediate potential

E-Commerce sales across Europe are growing fast. Since 2010 there has been a rapid rise in consumer switching to online purchasing and increasing signs of preference for that convenience + value. This has been fuelled by improvements all leading retailers and etailers have been making to their web site experience, consumer preference for integrated multi-channel shopping enabling them to browse, compare and buy, developments in broadband speed and Mobile, substantial investments in fulfilment and logistics enabling next day and even same delivery and increased confidence with online payment methods and security.

All this has led to double digit % growth in revenues in all the key markets and total online sales for 2014 in Europe expected to reach €200bn and forecast by a DirectCommerce to hit €300bn by 2018. Even slow to develop markets like Italy and Spain are now jumping on the e-commerce bandwagon and new online markets are quickly emerging in Eastern Europe with Russia leading that pack.

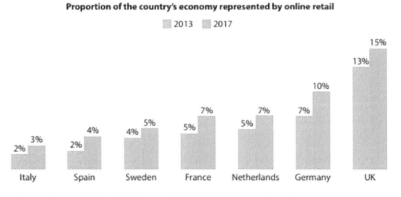

By 2017, Online Retail Will Be A Significant Part Of Many Countries' Economies

Proportion of the country's economy represented by online retail

2013   2017

Source: Forrester Research Online Retail Forecast, 2012 To 2017 (Western Europe)

Source: Forrester Research, Inc.

In a recent survey from ChannelAdvisor, 71% of retailers said that they are actively considering cross-border expansion using online as their first step, before any bricks 'n mortar investment. And while USA and BRIC markets attract because of their market size and the long term business potential, the proximity of Europe and ease of access makes continental expansion a natural first step overseas opportunity. IMRG estimate that cross-border online sales in Europe will reach €36bn in 2015 and that for UK (r)etailers c. 10% of online sales are already to customers outside the UK.

Here's what some are saying:

"International e-Commerce has become a priority for us. In 2015, we will be transactional in 10 countries. Investment is accelerating because we think this is a very big opportunity"

Marks and Spencer

"Boosting mulit-channel is at the heart of what we are doing, with George.com, we are launching an overseas digital offensive with plans to open up the George.com web site to 14 countries across Europe following the initial successful pilot in Ireland"

Asda

"Our plan is to "woo" Europe. We have seen a sharp rise in traffic to our UK web site from overseas customers, we have had international delivery in place for some time, but now we will launch local language sites in France and Germany to also accept payments in €uros".

John Lewis

"International expansion is a major factor in our growth. We are developing dedicated web sites and in-country teams… we plan to be the number one fashion destination in all our markets… we want customers wherever they log on to be able to buy and find local fashion that they want"

Asos.com

Most (r)etailers start their overseas expansion plans with some caution. History is littered with failed international expansion plans. So the key lesson is to start slowly and test the water. A possible roadmap might look like this:

■1. Use web analytic tools to track numbers of overseas visitors to the web site, eg numbers, growth, where from, what they buy, level of returns…

■2. Enable international delivery: For example, HarveyNichols.com still only allows for UK delivery and provides no offer or solution for someone who wants delivery in another country. Even Harrods.com was slow to introduce international delivery and payment capabilities. Many US web sites still do not allow for people outside the US to buy. As a result, a number of intermediary distributors have emerged such as Reship.co.uk and MyUS who will provide a US shipping address and then for a fee forward the parcel on to the UK.

JCrew.com is an example of a company that has recently addressed this by immediately identifying which country the visitor is from and offering its own local currency and local shipping solutions.

■3. Evaluate local market conditions and competitor environment: Local consumers may have different tastes and style, the obvious truism-what sells in one market may not sell in another.

The challenge is always about how stay true to the Brand's DNA while meeting local consumer preferences.

A classic example of what not to do comes from shirt retailer Charles Tyrwhitt who opened in Japan only to find that its typical shirt sizes were too big for the local market. Obvious, well, yes in hindsight, for sure, but at that time it was just overlooked amid the excitement and flurry of opening overseas. Now, that same company has learnt from these basic mistakes and has a highly successful overseas online operation driving nearly 50% of its sales.

Cycle retailer Wiggle.com also provides some good lessons: "we have a structured approach to expanding to new overseas markets. We run a base level of activity to start with that identifies which have the most potential and then we can begin to focus on those that respond best. We have a new market entry model which looks at local consumers and preferences, what their expectations are around the customer journey to take into account delivery expectations, payment methods, customer service, contact methods etc so that we can understand the local market complexities".

Hobbs, the fashion retailer, has taken a very planned and stepped approach: "Overseas returns take time and cost to manage and we feel the need to have a long term strategy and plan. We have worked through focus groups, desktop research and analysis of existing overseas sales patterns to prioritise where and how to best invest and build out online. There is no substitute for spending time in a local market, building relationships, understanding the customer, the culture and nuances. We believe that it can take 5 yrs to achieve real critical mass and target return on investment"

■4. Consider using "Market Places" to further test the waters.

Market Places are in fact playing a significant role in enabling (r)etailers to expand to overseas markets and reach new customers. Amazon and eBay lead the field with their huge global reach. Amazon has c.175 million active accounts worldwide and that has led to c. $75 billion in global revenues. eBay in fact has an even larger customer base worldwide estimated at c. 200 million. Both companies have been investing substantially and growing their third-party market place models. Others such as Tesco and La Redoute have been following in their footsteps also establishing online platforms for other retailers to sell through. Example is electronics retailer Maplin with their own storefront on Tesco Direct (linked to Tesco.com).

And key social media networks like Facebook also provide that storefront /shop window access though without any "Amazon-like" market place support.

In Japan, the market place model is very highly developed with some 60% of online consumers preferring to shop that way using eg Rakuten. And in South America, the Mercado Libre market place provides a similar trusted and preferred e-commerce portal.

Market Places like these are already established with consumers, they have high numbers of visitors to their web sites, they are trusted retail platforms and importantly they typically also have a developed warehousing and delivery infrastructure which is reliable and encourages further online buying. On-time and reliable delivery has become one of the most critical drivers of success for any online business these days and getting product efficiently to the consumer's door is no easy task. Amazon though can offer a ready-made service with a developed programme through their fulfilment centres and can provide warehousing, inventory control and delivery now to 26 European countries, as well as other key markets across the world.

■5. There is always a time for supplementing the online development with a local bricks' mortar presence, but many are now seeing traditional plans for stores in every large town as being unnecessary. The whole concept of multi-channel is to enable and provide the most cost-effective consumer experience and a few flagship stores in only the most major malls and cities need be considered. Marks and Spencer is certainly an example of such an approach. In the 1990's it opened up some 30 stores across France, the investment was considerable and ten years later a new management team shut them all down. Now M&S has returned to France but its focus is on the international customers more obviously centred around Paris and that will be its heartland in the short /medium term. (in fact M&S has also announced that will not open any more UK general merchandise stores "because of the growth in digital").

■6. Once the preliminary steps have proved encouraging then the growing e-commerce environment makes it quick and easy to expand:

- Karen Millen launched its foreign language web sites across Germany, France, Spain, Holland and Sweden, backed by a mix of own stores and concessions in key department stores. "we are keen to expand our international e-commerce as nearly two thirds of online sales already come from overseas".

- Made.com, the online furniture retailer backed by LastMinute's Brent Hoberman, has recently announced its expansion to establish its online business in France. "Logistically, France works for us as it's close to our UK warehousing. In addition, we ship from the Far East and delivery into UK or France has the same lead times so we feel we can continue to promise our fast service from order time to delivery to the home".

- while Boots has shops in Norway, Ireland, Netherlands and Thailand, only in 2014 did it announce the expansion of its *online* operation to international markets. The start is Ireland and then if that all goes well into northern Europe. "We are focussing on getting it right in Ireland first before opening up elsewhere. We will then use that as the platform for the wider international roll-out." (In the meantime, Boots.com saw sales rise nearly 20% year on year, and building this mulit-channel presence would appear to be critical with 45% orders being click 'n collect).

- River Island, BrandAlley, Hobbs, Mothercare, House of Fraser, Holland & Barratt are among a slew of UK retailers with plans to build out overseas through expansion online. "The online market is still immature, and especially outside the UK there is still "land to be grabbed"!

Of all the overseas markets that get considered, Germany consistently emerges as the most attractive and more than 64% of UK companies considering overseas expansion online named Germany as the market most likely to provide overseas sales growth and as their priority over the next 5 years. (research by

Barclays). Next and Arcadia are two retailers that have made Germany a key priority:

- more than 50% of shoppers in Germany will shop online
- total population of 80 million provides the largest potential in Europe
- online sales in 2013 amounted to c. €40bn and forecast to grow at c. 20% for several more years
- increasing popularity of smartphones and tablets is driving easier consumer access and enabling "shopping on the go" with 25% of shoppers going online via their mobile and 25% of that group saying that they complete the full shop via their mobile device. Research shows that behaviour pattern is becoming an increasing trend.
- the growth in B2B commerce online is also accelerating, creating a purchasing mindset which is all about the growing familiarity, convenience and ease of e-commerce and an expectation that that is the preferred way to shop
- a highly developed logistics infrastructure with Germany reckoned to be the most sophisticated in this respect. There are more than 3,500 national courier companies ranging from the big players like Deutsche Poste and DHL through to numerous small to mid-sized operators
- challenges include:
  - Managing a high rate of returns: "Germans are the return champions" with c. 40% of shoppers typically returning some items bought during their online shopping. These leads to rising demand and expectation around delivery, ability to return and the whole customer servicing, handling of complaints, the logistics around returns and refund management, the handling and distribution of returned merchandise and the costs of doing this.
  - Payment: Germans are not big users of credit cards online. Purchasing on account, PayPal and Direct Debit are the three most preferred payment solutions with c. 80% of online users stating these three methods as the ones they look for. This is important of course because expanding a UK site and expecting to build business in Germany will be severely limited if local payment options are not easily available online.

★★★★★

With so much opportunity and potential as e-commerce develops internationally, the key lessons learnt for how best to succeed can be summarised:

(i) *Language*: it's not enough just to translate the English web site. Someone local needs to review the translation to look for translation mistakes, misleading phrases and whether local culture and tastes are taken into account. "It's got to look and feel local otherwise we've learnt it just does not work"

Irish web site Siopa.com has had success in the US with its Irish-made crafts while its attempts to attract customers across Europe has done less well. At Siopa they concluded that part of the problem across Europe was that its brand name just did not "translate well whereas in the US, we found the name carried an Irish charm!" (Siopa is simply the Gaelic for shop).

(ii) *VAT /Sales tax*: there are of course different rules and regulations for how to charge this, whether to include it in the stated price or not, how to manage the tax payments with the local authorities. VAT registration is required in every country it's planned to ship to.

(iii) *Local Marketing*: ways to promote will vary by country. Some will respond better to direct mail than others. Some may prefer email. Some will want call centre support while others will be more self-serve. Promotion messages which attracted customers in one location may be found off-putting or distasteful or just culturally wrong in another.

(iv) *Affiliates*: each country will have its own comparison shopping engines, its own affiliate marketing programmes and establishing relations with these may become critical.

(v) *Search engines* will vary and key words may be different. Search Engine Optimisation algorithms will change in different countries and what works in one will not be the same as what works elsewhere. Optimising for search is something that's also critical to get right.

(vi)*Web content accessibility*: guidelines have been developed by the EU to enable better access for eg people who are visually impaired and expectations around how well this is implemented vary widely in different countries

(vii) *overall design and user experience*: this can be influenced by simple things like hair styles, appearance of the models used, the way products are merchandised, standards of photography, as well as by general look 'n feel.

(viii) *social media platforms*: will vary by country and for a business to succeed, building networks on local platforms can be a key and positive influence

(ix) *payment methods*: understanding the preferences around payment methods will be another deciding factor. In Germany, Sofortuberweising for example is a popular payment method, a kind of e-payments wallet similar to PayPal. In the Netherlands, they like something similar but local to them called iDeal. In France the preference is for Carte Bleue, the popular debit card payment system.

For UK businesses, used to working with credit/debit cards, then the other most developed card markets for online are Denmark, Norway, Switzerland and Spain

(x) *delivery*: often each country will have a local trusted logistics company and in the Netherlands for example research has shown that arranging delivery through PostNL does generate more trust and will increase sales and site conversion rates. In contrast in France, "drop points" or local pick-up locations is a common form of delivery where consumers have trust in eg a local store to take deliveries and hold them for the consumer to pick up when most convenient.

As an illustration: Activinstinct.com, the online sports goods store, launched in Germany and was surprised when most of its customer deliveries were returned. Many of its new customers had asked for delivery to a secure local locker for later pick up, but Activinstinct had overlooked the need to set up a separate contract with the local locker companies. So without that, the goods were simply "returned to sender". That early misfire caused some negative PR and took some time to overcome.

(xi) *local laws and regulations*: "At Kingfisher /B&Q we face distinct local and regulatory hurdles such as markedly different rules to set up domain names across the EU and numerous product merchandising and labelling regulations which despite apparent EU uniformity vary by country"

★★★★★

Like any new business opportunity, there can be significant potential while also significant challenges. Online is growing so fast and it is so obviously something that consumers are looking for that it is a very attractive investment option. What's helpful in 2014 and beyond is that the lessons are being learnt on how best to succeed, what to watch out for, what keys will drive success. It does seem that a measured and considered approach is more likely to build long term and sustainable success while managing levels of investment and risk and learning for each business what works and what will give the best RoI.

Chapter 17

B2B Social Media

There is growing recognition that social media can play a key role in B2B marketing. According to an e-Consultancy report B2B social media has reached a tipping point as it gradually becomes a mainstream tool for customer engagement and business development.

- Cisco recently decided it would use only social media to announce and market the launch of a new router product. This gave the opportunity to establish a wide-scale and immediately interactive environment where customers could look at video content and demos, ask questions, see what other customers were saying, arrange for a sales call, read through specs, participate in web and podcasts and generally engage. It has been acclaimed as one of Cisco's most successful ever launches. In addition this generated three times as much press coverage as their previous comparable product launch

- Dell has been developing its B2B social media now for several years and has learnt many lessons on its journey of how best to make that investment pay back. It now adopts "social media principles" in the way it engages with all its customers and also all its employees. It uses SM not just to communicate new ideas and plans but also to listen and learn so it can anticipate. Among other things it has a policy of actively monitoring all online brand conversations and turning those with negative views into advocates. It invites those people to its offices and assembly plants. It goes out of the way to make sure it addresses concerns as they arise and is proactive, not reactive, Dell say that as a result of this in the past year they achieved an incremental $25m of sales. "Our customers are more influenced by what other customers say than what we say. In the B2B world that connection is even more important"

- American Express has launched OPEN forum which is a place for SMEs to share comments and ideas about not just AMEX products but about all manner of SME type issues and concerns from bank borrowing, securing investment, tax, NI and a host of other things. "it's our equivalent of Mumsnet, it's a place where business people can see what are the hot topics of the day, share, learn and engage. We have found a significant increase in corporate customer business flowing directly from this channel"

- BT has had some similar success with TradeSpace which now has c.350,000 members and provides a general business social networking forum and place and which BT will use to announce new products and initiatives.
- Microsoft, HP, PayPal, RICS, UPS, RS Components are examples of other companies who are all taking positive steps to make social media work for their business customers.

A recent PWC survey also confirms that we are now looking at one of those "tipping points" where more and more organisations in the B2B space are now trialling, investing in and learning about how to make social media work for them.

Why is this? What's making this become a more important agenda item and opportunity?

It's not just the growing swell of examples and anecdotes in this area; it's also because of other factors:

(i) Mobile devices are enabling so much more connectivity. Prospective customers will be tweeting about a new product launch at trade shows or sharing immediate comment and observation about their reactions in online forums and it's crucial that the product company can monitor those conversation threads. And of course it's possible to proactively connect with those conversing and invite them to your trade show stand or for a follow-up demo and call.

(ii) Employees expect more and more to be able to work in an environment where they can interact and collaborate to solve problems and share ideas. Social Media is displacing the now "old-fashioned" Intranet.

(iii) Business audiences generally and buyers are influenced by the same forces that influence retail customers. Expectations are changing.

(iv) Those companies who are developing social media strategies are finding that it lifts their whole customer communication to much more engaging level.

Instead of somewhat dry and functional brochures and specs there can now be live and continuous human interaction.

(v) Cost reduction: in this climate of budget and cost consciousness companies like Cisco found that not only did their SM product launch work better than traditional ways of doing things but it was much more cost effective. It was also much more measurable and possible to determine exactly which elements generated the most leads.

With this area beginning to attract more and more attention, what are companies generally doing about it?

In its recent survey, PWC found that 48% of companies had appointed someone with at least part time responsibility for this SM area. 20% had appointed someone full time, 12% had set up a small team. Only 13% had no dedicated resource at all.

When the survey looked more deeply within organisations to explore what the workforce wanted, then 75% of people indicated they would like to see more social media deployment and through their company. This was as much about enabling and supporting peer to peer communications as it was about giving other opportunities and ways to connect and interact with existing and prospective customers.

What PWC and e-consultancy and other observers are also finding is that "dabbling" in SM activity is counterproductive. They liken it to the early days of companies going online when many were still unconvinced about the value or need for an online presence. Companies who approached that situation half-heartedly got minimal if no return. And worse still if not done well, then it led to poor customer experience and a negative outcome. What Dell and others have found is that a small but sensible level of resource can quickly pay back. And the gains are not just short term in terms of more business leads and potentially new revenues. The longer team gains of more vocal and considered customer support, the stronger Brand engagement and identity can lead to still further positives down the track.

Chapter 18

How should B2B companies be taking advantage of "Digital"

Can "digital" drive revenue growth for B2B? in past few years, it's B2C companies that have been pioneering e-commerce and online customer engagement. But there's now a growing number of B2B companies finding a lot of success and opportunity from a more assertive digital path.

And "digital" does not need to mean direct e-commerce sales. That is an option but there is a wealth of easy steps and initiatives that can be taken online and with mobile that can generate growth, without even having to offer that direct sales channel.

A key concern for B2B companies: will more direct customer dealing affect current supply relationships? How will our Sales teams react if they see the company also selling direct online? Do our end customers even want to connect and or buy direct online and bypass traditional channels?

The learning is that channel conflict *is* a concern but that it *is* manageable. And there are many examples now about how to do that. What's more, companies that go down this path are now regularly reporting incremental revenue growth of anything between 5 and 20%.

Companies from global multi-nationals like 3M, GE, Cisco and Reed Elsevier to smaller niche market operators like Farrow & Ball paints, IC International yarns and threads, Norgren fluid controls manufacturing, Bobcat Doosan construction equipment, Eden Springs water coolers, Pitney Bowes printer /office supplies... there is a growing list of B2B organisations, or companies with some B2B products /services, who are seeing success through moving more into "digital".

Here are some key facts:

1. 81% of Purchasing /Procurement Managers said they would choose a supplier that offers an online ordering option over an equal supplier who

does not. The reasons were: (i) do business at our convenience, (ii) save time, and (iii) easily monitor order status (Hybris survey).

2. B2B revenues transacted online, not through EDI, rose to close to £40bn in the UK and c. $300bn in the US.
   (that US figure is more than the $200bn recorded in the US for online B2C transactions).
   These figures are expected to double by 2018 (Forrester report).

3. 25% of B2B companies in a recent Oracle survey said they now sold direct using e-commerce

4. and 80% of companies in that survey said that they are now actively reviewing this opportunity, whether to launch or invest further,

5. Mobile has become a key catalyst with 68% of companies saying that this had changed the way distributors and customers wanted to connect and trade

6. B2B companies generally are acknowledging this growing potential of digital and generally predict that e-commerce will become 50% of total sales. A number are claiming average growth rates of up to 30% + (Forrester /JP Morgan report).

Some have described all this as "the consumerisation of B2B". The same B2B buyers /procurement managers have just moments before been eg on Amazon.com downloading books to their Kindle, streaming music or a movie, and using the immediate and simple "one-click" order process. These same procurement managers are personally connected up, use tablets, use smart phones, like the latest gadgets, have children constantly trying out new web sites and online ideas. All that sets expectations. That ease of access, ease of use, ease of purchasing becomes a way of behaving and operating. And it is fuelling demand from customers big and small who want the same business purchasing opportunities.

But at the same time as this "digital" pressure mounts, so the learning for companies is: don't rush into this. There is a clear templated approach that has now emerged that shows a roadmap, a path, a way to push ahead on this journey.

The key is that this is a series of steps and learnings. It's about how to get things moving, how to take advantage and the pitfalls to avoid. There are essentially 2 key stages:

1. **Pre-e-Commerce**: using digital to engage and interact with customers
2. **e-Commerce**: establishing a digital and multi-channel sales capability enabling customers to buy how and when they want to.

There's a great story from a recent Cisco Sales conference. The Sales team did its annual review and saw there was one new customer who had purchased nearly $100m of equipment, and it had all been done in automated manner online. There had been no call centre or Sales force contact. And so, naturally, the immediate reaction of the Sales team was right, let's get our key Sales guys down there, let's get connected. But the customer declined the Sales call. Said they were very happy thankyou and preferred the ease and convenience of the online self-serve order process. Don't worry they said, we'll email you if any issues do come up.

Let's have a look at **Stage 1: Pre-e-Commerce**. What steps can the company take to get more digitally connected with customers, to create interest in products and services, to differentiate from competitors, to make it easy for customers to engage and purchase even it's the actual buying process continues to be through "traditional" and established supply routes and channels.

There are 6 steps or specific opportunities and things that can be done. There is no prescribed order but here is a practical plan:

- SEO
- Key functional tools
- Data capture
- Generate leads for Sales team
- Account management /order tracking /customer portal
- Social media

Let's briefly consider each of these:

1. SEO: Search Engine optimisation.
This simply means that when existing or prospective customers are looking to find out latest news, products available, which suppliers to contact, then a search

on Google or other search engine will rank your company and its products to the top of page one.

And this is so important because research shows that searchers only occasionally go beyond that first page. And it's an easy thing to test:

For example a global B2B multi-national was looking to boost its digital market presence. They operated in the threads and yarns. But type in "threads and yarns" in Google and they were nowhere to be seen. Many of their key competitors however did appear on the list. Alongside a number of new niche more agile, "digitally aware" rivals. Bottom line, this company was getting no leads or enquiries through its online presence. While a rival proclaimed in its annual results that "new investment in digital has added significantly to our growth prospects".

And this is not difficult or costly to fix. There are now many SEO consultancies and experts who can work to optimise a web site presence. (type in SEO agency and you'll get a highly competitive list of the best, on page 1!).

2. Key functional tools:

www.pitneybowes.com provides a whole suite of functions that enable customers to "self-serve". For example they can request a brochure, access detailed product specifications, contact the PB Technical centre by email or call to get technical advice, read case studies that show how PB customers have used new workflow solutions to cut costs, get a quote, ask for a Sales department call back… all things that can be done at the customer's convenience and accessible from any device, via desktop PC, tablet or mobile.

www.bt.com/selfserve is aimed at Business customers. Its target is to "empower and enable our customers to get the best from BT". As well as offering a range of functions, it offers an AutoConnect self-serve product that enables its own B2B customers to offer "self-serve" digital solutions.

3. Data Capture

This simply means that whoever visits your site, you would ideally like to get their contact details as they may be a future customer or an existing customer who might have some questions before placing their next order. So this is simply about collecting that contact information. Simple idea, surprising rarely done proactively, and when done, then often not very well.

But what data is needed? Just an email address is all. Just a simple email address. How many times have we clicked on "Contact us" pages and found instead a long form to fill in. Immediate reaction is negative and there is often no wish to spend time filling it in or giving all that information. For example, one global insurer offering home insurance had a 3 page initial contact us form. Among other things asking for make and technical description of the home central heating system. Needless to say very few people completed the form.

It's all about the "value exchange". I will spend time filling in forms, only if I will get some immediate value back. Make it easy to leave an email address and the number of potential follow-up opportunities will increase.

Some companies eg Microsoft, Samsung will pop up a window after 2 minutes on the site, or just when the visitor exits with a "Thank you for visiting" message and an invitation to leave email address for follow-up contact information. And today, with cookies and behavioural targeting it is possible to have tracked that visitor experience and send a more personalised and targeted follow-up email with product relevant information.

4. Generate leads for the Sales force

Tyco, ADT, Cisco, Xerox, Sony Business all have for a number of years used their online presence specifically as a lead generator. And their web sites are all geared to that one particular goal.

This can be critical because many companies try to get their web sites to do lots of things. From providing news, investor info, press releases, latest results, brand imagery, videos, meet the CEO, long lists of products and services. And all fighting for attention and space on a crowded homepage.

The better digital companies have all been through that. They are further on the journey. They have learnt about simplicity and single-mindedness. Surely what's key, especially in today's more challenging economic conditions is to find every opportunity to drive sales. So why not get the web site to work hard for that.

www.adt.com/commercial is a good example. www.sony-europe.com/pro now has a well-oiled engine to capture data leads and deliver same day follow-up. JSP Manufacturing www.jsp.co.uk has a strong multi-channel approach combining call centre and fast online response. They have won recognition and awards for their online innovation.

5. Account management /order tracking /customer portal

www.solutions.3M .co.uk has on its main navigation bar a key tab: Partners and Suppliers. This leads to a series of partner, supplier and customer-facing account management /relationship-building initiatives. There is B2B Portal which product lists the entire 3M range of >5 million order lines and enables all ordering to be done online. There is the 3M Order Centre which enables customers to check status of orders and invoices. There is the 3M Extranet which provides dedicated and personalised customer and supplier documentation and account information. In addition there are optional facilities such as automated change requests, FAQs and workforce solutions.

6. Social media

A recent PWC B2B survey showed that social media as a means for strengthening business customer relations had reached a "tipping point". 48% of companies in the survey said they either had already appointed or planned to appoint an in-house Head of Social Media. Companies like Dell, PayPal, UPS, HP and many others were all quoted in the survey as saying that their engagement with social media forums and discussions had "materially contributed to revenue gains".

Dell is a now well-known case study. In 2013 they tracked some $40m of sales directly as a result of "social media listening". Dell proactively participates in consumer as well as business user and prospective customer forums whether on Facebook, Twitter, Wired, PC Guide, CNET or any number of a dozen other widely trawled discussion sites. Dell has dedicated in-house people who monitor and contribute, and deal with complaints. "We turn critics into advocates". Dell estimates there are 25,000 daily social media mentions around the globe that are relevant and could impact their revenue line, positively or negatively. So "active monitoring pays back".

American Express "Open Forum" for business, RS Components, HSBC, Virgin Group Pioneers forum for new and small /mid-sized businesses… are all finding that this has become a key source of customer and prospective customer interaction

★★★★★

In summary, this Stage 1 "pre-e-commerce" opportunity is already rich in opportunity. B2B companies are hiring experts from the B2C world to apply their learning and experience in their own markets. The principles are the same even if the target customer is different. And this can all be done within existing supplier relationships. It's all about building the Brand in the digital age and making a mark. And many of these initiatives can be established easily and at relatively low cost.

One immediate action step that many are pursuing is to appoint a Head of

Digital or if especially determined then a Chief Digital Officer. This person /role acts a champion for digital, a focal point for new ideas and activities, a driver of change and someone who can set out the both the strategy and roadmap that can start to deliver some of these benefits.

★★★★★

What then about stage 2? If a company has set up its digital stall and found the good progress that others have in being "digitally assertive", then it is likely ready to explore and move things to the next level.

There are another 5 steps on the journey. And each is designed to let the organization learn, get comfortable and get ready for further activity.

- Trials and samples
- Specialist e-comm sales
- Mobile
- Full range e-comm sales
- True multi-channel

Here is a wonderful example of how one company embarked on this stage 2 e-commerce venture:

Procter & Gamble has long sold through established and often large scale distributors. This has been their way of operating both in their consumer as well as in their own B2B product initiatives. The distributors could be Wal-Mart, Walgreens, Tesco or specialist distributors for their Oleochemicals, but they are often powerful intermediaries in their own right. And alongside that, P&G has large sophisticated Sales teams of its own with major distribution sales relationships.

But in 2009, P&G started asking the obvious question: with the growing power of the internet, surely we should be connecting direct with our customers? For example, we do already encourage them to call us if there is a product problem and we fix it even if the product was bought at Wal-Mart. And if a customer cannot find a specific flavour or variant then we will supply direct. And we have a large B2B Business where customers are increasingly looking to us to provide online functions and support.

So P&G embarked on a "get digital" programme. They went through all of stage 1 described here. But once that was in place and as the importance of digital continued to grow there was desire among all to do more.

Among others things P&G then set up its own e-commerce store: www.pgestore.com. The aim was to sell certain selected low key / end of range /surplus stock. It was done carefully and with full communication to all distributors. It was set up as a natural evolution from Stage 1 above. It focussed on product lines and SKU that were typically not stocked by the big distributors or rarely or were low margin or large bundled product solutions and all executed in a way that there would be negligible if any impact on distributor sales. The supply chain accepted the need and importance for P&G to use online to build its brand, enhance customer satisfaction and in doing so establish a multi-channel presence which would reinforce distributors' own sales and promotion efforts. P&G put a lot of effort into distributor communication.

Bottom line P&G's eStore works. In 2013, sales were c. $500m. It's expected to double by end 2015. It's still only available in the US but it's likely to move slowly out to international markets. All with same step-by-step careful and selective open communication approach.

P&G and others believe that while this is a pioneering time and while distributors are getting used to this multi-channel world then it is still a time for this carefully managed development. But that by 2018 this will be the norm, it will be accepted, it will be the way things get done.

Sales force teams are also in the process of operating in this multi-channel way and incentive and revenue recognition structures are being put into place to make sure the Sales person does not feel disenfranchised.

Samsung, GE, Philips and many others all have strong multi-channel offerings. Many now have a "how to buy" navigation tab which offers all the routes: "distributor finder", phone us, order direct online, contact us for a Sales call back etc. And they are all learning how to make this work, how to grow in confidence, how to build out the range of activities and the size of the product range on offer, how to manage distributors and keep the Sales team on side, how to gradually evolve so that they do gain from this online world and use it to advantage. Companies are beginning to realise that if they don't do it then rivals will and that the "land grab" for digital recognition and connection is happening now!

Chapter 19:

Digital check-list for making it happen!

In this new era of digital innovation and adventure, it is now much more challenging for a Brand to engage with its customers. In the "good old days", there were relatively few choices. There were three main channels of engagement and distribution:

- Above the line (ATL): meant a mix of TV (if the brand budget could afford it), typically some press/print and if feeling bold a radio ad.
- Below the line (BTL): leaflet/sample distribution to people's homes
- In-Store: point of sale incentives and information

A brand marketing team was used to that set of choices. Agencies were skilled at understanding those specific options and the work load could be divided between two or three agencies: one for the ATL, one for the BTL and one for other stuff! But now, as the twenty first century gathers pace, it's all become a lot more complicated. At the last count there were at least 30 different channel and communication options:

Multi-channel options

TV broadcast 30" or interactive, Cinema (3-D or not 3-D?), Radio, Print, Mobile ad or content sponsorship, apps for smart phones, apps for tablets like iPad, pod casts/vod casts, Bluetooth mobile, Direct Marketing, e-mail, catalogue, telemarketing, sales reps, poster, outdoor/event, kiosks, vending, PR, Social Media, Sponsorship, In-game advertising, Point of sale, In-store, on cart, website, online advertising, Search, viral video, affiliates…

It's become a bit of a dinner party game these days to see if you can identify any others! There is just a bewildering array of choice for any brand marketing team and an almost impossible set of decisions about channel mix, budget allocation, which channels to prioritise, which can be ignored. In addition, the audience that a Brand must reach has now become fragmented and widely dispersed and does not consume media in the easy-to-reach passive way that they used to.

TV, once the home of mass audience reach, is now fragmented and unreliable. It has soared from a few mainstream channels to many hundreds. It's available live or in catch up, via cable or satellite, via internet-connected TV or even down the broadband phone line. People no longer just watch right through a programme. They can skip through ad breaks eg on Sky + or Tivo. They multi-task and might have one eye on the TV set, another on their Facebook page and also be watching for tweets and emails on Twitter and/ or speaking with friends via Skype or instant messaging. Engaging with this audience in the most efficient and effective way has become mesmerising and complex:

- which channels deliver the best ROI?
- which campaigns work best on which channels?
- if we communicate via channel A then is there a "must-have" complementary channel B that also needs to be involved?
- is there an ideal channel mix?
- can we "afford" to ignore eg social media or mobile?
- or could we "afford" to ignore expensive TV and switch to apparently lower cost online?
- does the channel mix vary by season?
- is there a different channel mix for different target customer segments?
- given that it's all changing so fast and new channel opportunities are emerging, how can we check that what we plan for this year is going to be relevant and appropriate?

The start of an answer to these questions is to best understand what the target customer prefers. But such research can be time-consuming and expensive and would need to ideally cover all types of segments and audiences and like a lot of research may well be inconclusive. So how about an easy top-down approach?

6 step test: a brand check for the digital multi-channel age?

Here's a quick 6 step test to see how far your Brand has already travelled in moving away from traditional media channels and becoming more of a digital multi-channel brand. Each of these steps uses free tools and analysis. They are quick and easy to do.

1. *Go to Adwords.google.com/targeting*
   Type in the name of your brand and you will get an instant analysis of monthly traffic, global and local searches as well as any click through analysis if the brand is being advertised on Google already

2. *Go to Google.com/insights/search* and you can see the traffic analysis over time, last year, last week as well as related content/articles that might be influencing those search levels, you can also search at local, country or global level

3. *Now go to Alexa.com* and you can look up your web site and start to get comparative traffic data looking at your brand site versus others in your category. It shows how high the web site ranks in terms of traffic generation. And amazingly, there is a whole consumer demographic and segmentation analysis that tells you eg: by age, gender, education, family and location.
   It will also tell you where your web site traffic is coming from so you can work out eg if your Brand is say Pepsi, that the number 1 connecting site in UK is Sky Sports. That will tell you about existing campaign effectiveness, which ads working which not (eg the ads on Yahoo are not working). But will also start to give you a lot more info on the size and type of your online audience
   You can begin to start understanding whether and to what degree your Brand is participating in this digital world

4. *Next go to Facebook.com* and at the search facility type in your brand name. You will immediately find the number of Facebook fans and friends you have. Again you can type in competitor brands and see what their numbers are. Is your Brand being left behind in the social media race? Or is this whole category just not of sufficient interest for people to want to talk about it And even more helpfully, you can find out what people are saying about

your brand, good and bad. And a similar exercise can be carried out on Twitter.com where the postings and tweets and number of followers can be very immediate and responsive to any marketing or advertising activity.

5. *Next, go to Technorati.com* where again for free you can use their Search facility which will review the "blogosphere" and find all recent and current blogs about your Brand or any related topic of interest.(www.twingly.com provides a similar search and functionality).

6. if you want *"a one search find all approach", then go to www.socialmention.com* which will trawl through the Net "searching content from across the universe" as they say. They will look at all blogs, news, video, audio and images.You can sort by date and by source. It will tell you where comment is coming from and what are the "buzz words" that are generating that comment. But most helpfully, they will also give you a "Sentiment score".
    -   This will tell you number of mentions which are positive, negative or neutral.
    -   It will also give you an overall sentiment score (ratio of positive to negative comment).
    -   there's also a Strength of Sentiment score, which is the percentage likelihood of the brand being discussed in a social media environment
    -   there's a Passion score which is the percentage likelihood that people talking about your brand will do so repeatedly
    -   lastly there's a Reach score which is a range of influence metrics and identifies the number of unique authors referencing the brand divided by the total number of mentions. That will help check if it's a few people mentioning you a lot or many with just a casual interest.

This tool will even give a list of the internet names of the top users/people who talk about this brand and give you a link to them. It's a wonderful way of getting in touch with people who could be or could become key influencers, who may themselves have lots of friends on Facebook and followers on Twitter and themselves can set the tone and reaction to how a product is perceived and rated.

And all this is for free! And there are other analytic tools like this eg Filtrbox which is now owned by Jive Software. Here you can get a free trial but unlike Social Mention, they have understandably taken a more commercial approach where you are required to sign up for the free trial and they will then look to convert you into a customer paying for the daily/weekly or monthly "buzz monitoring". Their analysis is presented in a more graphical format so can look easily too at patterns over time and compare with key competitors. Radian6.com and Infegy.com provide a similar service.

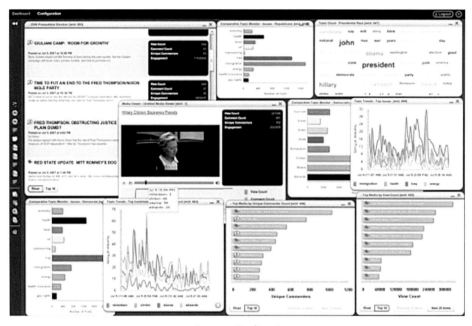

Source: Radian6

Yet another example, still for free, is Addictomatic. This site enables you to custom build and create your own web page with blocks of content regularly updated taken from Bing news feeds, Google blog search , Facebook, Twitter, YouTube, Instagram and Friendfeed.

And there are any numbers of software companies and brand consultancies offering for a fee to look at these brand monitoring sites and provide a report of what is going on out there in the digital world, how digitally engaged is the brand audience, how responsive generally is your product market or sector to a multi-channel approach, are there any learnings from what competitors are up to and, without too much analysis, how important are social, mobile and the other multi-channels becoming for short and medium term sales and marketing planning.

Some Brands have assumed that they are just not relevant enough to generate much social comment. They thought they would be largely untouched by the digital and multi-channel age. But that view can be violently disturbed especially if something goes wrong. Here's a case study which received such prominence that it became headlines in the New York Times, Huffington Post and countless other media places. It shows how the consumer has become more and more an influence on brand destiny and having a "multi-channel" strategy in place is just about essential for any brand, especially one operating in the highly competitive B2C spaces.

When two Dominos Pizza employees filmed a prank in the restaurant's kitchen, they decided to post it online ontoYouTube. It showed them messing about with the food. But within just a few days they found themselves on the end of a felony charge. And Dominos had more than a million disgusted viewers and faced a public relations crisis. What happened?

Within 48 hours of being posted online, the video had been viewed more than a million times. References to it were in five of the 12 results on the first page of Google search for "Dominos," and discussions about the film had spread throughout Twitter.

As Domino's began to realize, social networking has the reach and speed to turn local incidents into nationwide marketing crises. But they are not alone. Amazon for example was forced into an embarrassed apology in the same week for a "ham-fisted" error after Twitter members complained that the sales rankings for gay and lesbian books seemed to have disappeared — and, since Amazon took a few days to respond, the social-media world criticized it for being uncommunicative.

Back to Domino's, in just a few days it found its reputation significantly damaged. "It became a nightmare… the toughest situation for a company to face in terms of a digital crisis." Domino's Head Tim McIntyre was alerted to the videos by a blogger who had seen them. Bloggers at Consumerist.com used clues in the video to find the franchise location. They spread that news and forced the franchise to bring in the local health department. And local health advised that all the stock of food be thrown away.

As the company learned about the video, Domino executives initially decided not to respond very much, hoping the controversy would quiet down. "What we missed was the perpetual mushroom effect of viral sensations… in social media, if you think it's not going to spread, that's when it gets bigger… at the start we didn't know how to make our voice heard in that world"

After a few days, Domino's did create its own Twitter account to address the comments, and it presented its chief executive on YouTube. "It elevated to a point where just responding isn't good enough… we had to develop a full blown response both off *and* online using PR for the press and writing up almost every hour how things were progressing. It was a shock but you can be sure that now we monitor our brand, on all relevant channels, all the time, so we can react. But we also do this proactively to let the world know about the good things we are doing too!"

As Warren Buffet has said:" it takes 20 years to create a brand and twenty minutes to ruin it... if you think about it like that then you will certainly do things very differently!"

And so the message is that brand marketers need now to think and plan for their Brand for this multi-channel world. Even if some initial analysis suggests that the Brand is indeed not one that is typically gossiped and commented on, one bad PR mix up, in any channel, and as the folk at Dominos saw, reputations can come crashing very quickly.

Chapter 20

Case studies: building a successful online business- lessons learned

Three key questions drive this chapter:

1. What's required to build a growing, profitable and sustainable online business?
2. What marks out the winners?
3. What are the lessons learnt?

We can look at a number of outstanding case studies. Some products and services will lend themselves naturally and easily to online marketing and selling. Others can be harder to establish. But what comes through clearly is that there are no barriers, there is no reason why any brand or business organisation, no matter what sector it competes in, cannot achieve significant growth through online channels.

To understand this potential further, there has been considerable interest in what's called the "e-test". It looks at a brand's basic characteristics and identifies an "e-propensity score". Brands with high scores are considered to have a high likelihood of online success and if you get those high scores then you know you need to act immediately! These typically include products that can be simply presented in 2D on a page and where the purchase decision is based on an intelligent assessment of factors like price and availability. So services, like buying insurance and airline tickets, simple to present products like a book, a CD, a DVD can immediately be identified. You don't really need to visit a shop or meet someone to evaluate whether this is a product you would like to buy, especially if you know already what you want. But what if you get a low "e-propensity score"? Does that mean no customer interest in online communications and sales?

The purpose of this section is to review a number of case studies, to check whether "e-propensity scores" still matter and to look at the key lessons learnt to get some potential tips for future success.

•Case Study 1: TripAdvisor

On TripAdvisor you can book flights, hotels and restaurants. It provides coverage of every major destination across the globe. It will check other travel intermediaries like Expedia, Opodo, Orbitz, eDreams and consolidate the information from every airline flying for eg the designated departure airport to any destination. And the search engine is operating increasingly close to real time (though data updates vary depending on real time news feeds from each airline). The amount of data being crunched in each search is considerable and yet it's done in just a few seconds. What's more it provides reviews, ratings, testimonials from consumers, search comparison by price, by time, by airline, by date. There are also search alerts so you can be told about availability or relevant news updates, you can link in via Facebook so you and your pals could book online together and now you can also access the site in specially configured form via your mobile, search for a local hotel (the site can identify via GPS on your mobile where you are eg "find me nearest accommodation"), compare reviews and Book Now! It now operates in 14 languages across 23 countries worldwide and covers 24,000 destinations attracting 60 million visitors each month.

And when was TripAdvisor first launched? Just in 2000. And launched at the time when in fact Web 1.0 was bust, when the internet bubble was bursting, when doomsayers were saying there's no future for businesses on the Internet, when naysayers, like my friends at Argos at that time!, even if they could acknowledge the consumer convenience and benefits, would never invest anything significant.

What the founders of TripAdvisor have demonstrated is *how* you can build a substantial business on the Net. They aimed to become the "category killer". They wanted to be the destination brand that everyone went to. They asked how can we be that "first port of call"? They found backers in Flagship Ventures in Cambridge, Mass, in 2000 who were themselves passionate about online and believed in its long term potential. They gave the management team the time and the commitment to build a technically complex and demanding web site environment that could manage the huge number of real time data feeds and align that with a sophisticated search engine. What TripAdvisor does today has become more commonplace and easier to achieve but it does still take a lot of time, commitment and ingenuity to get there.

Payback came in 2005 with the sale to IDC who immediately put TripAdvisor together with Expedia. IDC have continued to invest and reports suggest they have put in a further $350m to get the site to the global, multi-country scale it is today. Last year it reported revenues moving closer to $1bn and profits of more than $300m and it's expecting continued high levels of growth as it neatly mixes social comment, advice and recommendations with an easy to use booking reference engine. Latest conservative valuations put it at more than $12bn! though some commentators suggest that still undervalues the "social community" aspects and its continuing ability to attract millions of visitors, its brand name or its category-killing status.

•**Case Study 2: Amazon**. Why have they been so successful? There are 3 key reasons:

(i). first and foremost it's simple, single-minded idea and highly functional. Type in name of book, film, music etc and up comes a ranked list. The format and presentation has hardly changed since it first launched.

(ii). it's very very easy to use. One click and you can buy. You can complete a transaction in seconds. I have often commented on this functionality. It is exactly what internet buyers are looking for. The general internet mantra is "quick, easy and convenient". If a site experience can past that test then it's got the core platform to succeed. Sounds straightforward, where's the complexity of that? But how many other sites offer a one-click functionality? They will ask you to log-in, remember your user name and password and often expect you to complete all the credit card details all over again. And even if you can get through that then you are often shunted off to some Visa verification site where you're expected to remember yet another password. But hang on, I've visited and bought from this site before, why can't they be like Amazon and just remember me?

The more clicks the visitor has to make to complete a purchase the more likely they will not complete and will abandon the shopping cart. Most abandon rates are typically between 40 and 80% which is already alarmingly high. How did you manage to lose a customer who had got that far into the process where they had liked what they saw, selected it, got ready to buy it and then 40 to 80% drop out! With Amazon one-click, you can see how that loss in minimised. One click and they've already bought! But research shows that more than 3 clicks and consumers start to get frustrated, after 6 clicks there are significantly diminishing returns and after 12 clicks, the rate of abandon quickly hits the 80% plus mark.

So why would anyone design a click-heavy site?

Extraordinarily, in this fast changing and competitive landscape, Amazon still stand out a mile in this respect. Not surprisingly they have seen off usurpers like Bookseller, Waterstones, Borders outside of the US, and Bertelsmann Bol.com, all of whom have flirted and tried to compete with Amazon's core book product line and failed to grab any significant market share.

"Easy to use" should be something every site now scores well on. But they don't. We can continue to see long lists of "worst web sites". Many especially B2B companies continue to put out "brochureware" with no purpose. Visitors can find pictures and sometimes even videos but if they'd like to contact someone at the company to make a purchase then there's no email address, no phone number, no names, just bland information. What's the point? How is a company going to get any RoI on its digital presence? What *is* the point? How much business /sales leads are they losing? Who is the site designer that put this together and thought this was a good idea? Who paid for it and why did they not ask the fairly simple and obvious questions? Why does this happen? Why do the obvious mistakes keep occurring?

(iii) The third test is that the "page must load immediately" (and countless research reports from Forrester make this point). Why is this so important? According to Forrester:

- 57% of consumers will abandon a web site if the page does not load within 3 seconds
- estimates are that a company can lose c.50% of its potential online sales if its pages don't load quickly
- for every second of delay in page loading, the viewer will spend less time looking at the page once it does load and in particular will not absorb any secondary promotional content or links

●Case Study 3: MyFaveShop.com

A couple of years ago, I observed at first hand a new e-commerce venture which became called MyFaveShop.com. The idea could be described as follows:

It was all about "social shopping". As you browsed the web you could click on anything you liked. It might be an item of clothing, an intended present, a Xmas list. Instead of that appearing in a long Favourites list, you could capture the image and the product detail and put that into your own specially designed shop. You could then invite friends to see your "collection", all laid out in a 3-D like retail store environment. And you could decorate and furnish that store in your own style. So you could say, put together a group of 4 or 5 dresses or coats you liked and had plans to buy one for the season. You could invite your friends to look at them and get their opinion on what would suit best. And then, if you wanted you could click and buy.

The core idea was "shopping together", co-browsing so you could look at the same screen together remotely in real time (eg ask sister Edith in Australia if she thinks this dress would suit Mum currently wintering in sunny Florida!)

But however nice the idea, it has taken a couple of paragraphs here to describe and illustrate. And therein lies its complexity. In contrast, Amazon takes one very short sentence to define: look at a list of products, select and buy. MyFaveShop however involved a lot of ideas and messages and because it was new and there was nothing like it at the time to benchmark or compare it required a lot of explanation to people visiting the site for the first time. How define in one short sentence what this was about?

So when this came to developing the simple, easy to use web site and navigation things got complicated. There was a whole variety of messages and explanations and illustrations all vying for prominence on the home page. Each member of the team had their own judgement on what should be the order and the priorities. The investors had their own marked preferences too. And even the consumer research that was conducted proved inconclusive. Some liked the idea, others didn't and each picked up on different aspects of the proposition:

- "I like the idea of social shopping"
- "design your own shop… that's cool"
- "put all my favourite things in one place"
- "create a wish list of things I want"
- "looking together at the same screen"
- "I like the choice of shop designs and being able to paint and furnish it how I like"

To complicate things further, it was clear that some visitors to the site would be web savvy and would "get" the concept quickly, need little hand-holding and want to get on with the site experience. While others would need more show and tell and so need an introduction and explanation. And finally, there had quite clearly to be an income stream so it was important that visitors got the message that they could browse and buy. At the same time there were key ad messages from brands that had to be found space and get incorporated!

The web team started to get very bogged down in the detail and trying to find the right web experience. Does the home page lead with the introductory explanation and even a step-by-step video or does it offer a navigation which tries to tempt all the different types of users and visitors. And what about repeat visitors? How get them engaged enough to register in the first instance? What type of data capture should be requested? At what stage in the visit is registration best requested?

The web site did launch, struggled out of Beta and was eventually and somewhat mercifully sold for a price, that at least gave some return, to another e-commerce organisation, who themselves found they were gradually forced to simplify things and in the end it became more and more like just another shopping web site.

It was a shame because there were some great ideas here and if the messaging challenge had been solved, if the right prioritisation had been found, if the user experience had been put together in a simple and easy to use form, if the investors had had more patience (or is that indulgence!), if the team had been able to cut through the complexity and for example found a way to start with just one big idea while adding other complementary messages and functions later, then this could, perhaps, have been a winning web site. But the learnings here from a disappointing experience can be just as compelling as ones about a successful one!

Simplicity is without doubt a virtue when it comes to designing web sites, content for mobile, Apple apps or any other stuff for a screen. That "home page" is a small piece of real estate, it's precious, the people who look at it are typically impatient and expect something quick, easy to digest, intuitive and arranged in such a way that they can very very easily make a decision to invest in this experience or click away. Most web sites have overall "fall-off rates" of over 90% from their home page. In other words most never make it to page 2. Why have Google and Facebook been so quick to catch on? While there may be many reasons, part of the explanation lies in their beautiful simplicity. You know immediately and unequivocally what they are all about.

Why is user experience simplicity so crucial? Research from Forrester and others highlights the following:

- they found that most people, if they could not immediately, within 3 seconds, understand what the site was about then they would leave.
- 8 out of 10 people will not revisit a site after a disappointing experience.
- in today's instantly networked social world, 35% of those who did have a disappointing experience say they will proactively tell friends not to visit that site.
- research from the Aberdeen Group shows that a 1 second delay in page load times equals 11% fewer page views, a 16% decrease in visitor satisfaction and a 7% loss in conversion. And as an example, Shopzilla improved average page load times from 6 seconds to 1.23 seconds and experienced a 25% increase in page views and a 12% increase in revenues.
- more than 60% of mobile users who visited brand web sites, found that mobile access was slow and information on the screen cluttered and sometimes unreadable.

●Case Study 4: General Motors

In general, 58% of people research a product or service provider online before buying according to PC Mag. In the auto sector that % goes up to 82% according to AutoTrader. Buying a car is a complex decision-making process as buyers compare and contrast models, review specs, read brochures, look at video content showcasing the car and the driving experience, and that's well before they've visited the showroom. Further research has shown that the auto sector is unlike other high ticket value items. With say the buying of a new TV set, consumers will use online to narrow down to a couple of different brands eg the "Sony Bravia" and the "Samsung UE55F". With research into cars however, people will use online to decide which brand they are going to buy and they will prioritise one only eg I'm going to buy a Ford and then will have in mind a couple at most of different model options. So online is even more critical in the auto sector. Make the online experience compelling and you drive your prospective customer right to your selected brand dealer showroom.

What the research goes on to say is that almost noone (there are exceptions) will buy a car site unseen and without "kicking the tyres", but even though the brand web site doesn't "sell" anything, its influence is still just as "mission critical".

General Motors in the US were one of the first car manufacturers to really understand the value of online. Inspired by examples from digital agency Modem Media, GM created MyGm.com. It was a place for the GM enthusiast.

Find out more about cars and get access to much more than you'd find on the basic web site. Register for news and invitations to special events and opportunities to drive the latest cars. It was also where the owner could register details of their own car, get reminders of services, get latest model upgrades and changes etc. It was one of the first very successful online loyalty-driving programmes which worked and although a bit clunky in 1999 it won a lot of acclaim among GM target customers.

And GM has not given up on it! Years later and it still provides a strong community environment for GM owners.

•Case Study 5: Clothing

All the early research showed that clothing would be one of the least successful areas to go online. After all people really want to feel the cloth, see what it looks like, try it on, examine the fit, check it goes with other items, it's a very visual, tactile and sensory buying experience. But, what we have found is that people do enjoy buying clothes online. And it's not just because it may be easier to find a special size but just because it's convenient. And now indeed with Facebook you can find ways to share and explore shopping ideas with friends and get advice on what to buy (who needed MyFaveShop!). Here are just a few examples of how successful online clothing sales have become:

- Asos.com has become an online fashion phenomenon. Its share price quadrupled since its launch in the space of just 18 months. It reaches customers all over the world, sales continue to increase at 20% to 30% plus and profits at the last results announcement were up 59%

- Clothing leads Online retail growth in China (Interfax China)
- "Gap Inc. pins growth hopes on online clothing sales". "Apart from high expectations for online in our core markets, we are launching our site for Japan and feel our brand gives us a great platform"
- From a piece of Deloitte research: "As retailers improve their web sites' visual merchandising and as the returns service generally gets more efficient, so we are reaching a tipping point in clothing especially among the 25 to 34 age group. This age group tend to live their lives online via smart phones and social networks. And that's why we've seen a number of leading retail clothing groups continuously improving their smart phone shopping apps."
- From a piece of Google research: "while tactility remains a purchase barrier for some, there is growing confidence in buying clothing online from trusted brands and especially for everyday wear such a shirts and repeat type purchases such as underwear".

What this success proves once and for all is that there are just no barriers to online success. Any product or service item can be made to work. It's just down to good old basic principles of understanding your market place and your customers and giving them what they want when they want it. Even fresh food is a growth sector in online shopping baskets and was the "fastest growing sector online for Tesco.com", albeit off a low base. In today's time-pressed world, time saved is highly valued.

●Case Study 6: global law firm.

If there are no limits on B2C, then what about the B2B arena? It's been argued that services which are complex, like legal services, are just not appropriate for an online world. Many lawyers felt that if a client wanted to decide which law firm to choose, or get expert advice then that could only be done with face-to-face contact and building a personal relationship. In fact so arrogant were most law firms that they hardly bothered with a web site and many just put up a token piece of brochure ware. However, even law firms, no matter how high end and sophisticated have belatedly begun to realise that the online world might just, just, be a little more important!

Here's an example from a top 10 global law firm. They had seen profit pressures due to market competitiveness. Some redundancies had been made but mostly to ensure and protect levels of partner profitability, which remained high. In this context, the firm had not developed its online presence beyond a fairly basic web site. But many in the law firm did not think that improving or investing in the site or more generally online would be worthwhile. How many people visit the web site and certainly how many would be influenced by it? Surely it was all about personal recommendations and personal networks, this online stuff had no relevance. And as for things like a strong presence on search engines or a social media strategy to engage with potential new staff trainees and associates from school, well, that was something for the likes of Coca-Cola, "not us".

However, a new marketing director had been hired who instinctively felt that the web had more influence and so some simple market research was conducted. Let's go talk to our target customers and actually ask them, direct, are they influenced by what they see online?

The answer that came back stunned the lawyers. After all they don't expect to get things wrong. But the research findings were absolutely based on what their new target clients were saying. The message back was loud and clear and more or less unanimous:

"for us, the web is the firm's window on the world… it's the first place we go to rather than look at brochures or fancy white papers… we expect a certain standard online, the kind of standard we'd expect from a top law firm… if we don't see that then we're going to start wondering if what we see online reflects the quality of the advice we'll get offline"

"yes, in something so personal and complex as legal advice we'd usually want to meet the firm and people we're going to work with… but when we're deciding on the pitch list we will do our due diligence and we find that starts with the web site"

"we don't mind slick, we don't mind a bit cheesy but we do expect class"

"yes, if I visited a firm's site and did not get a good and positive impression then it would change my mind about using them"

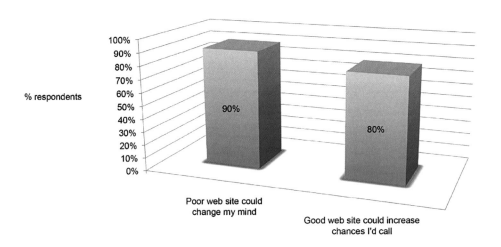

The firm's web site was appalling. The home page for example featured an interview which was nearly 2 years old with a partner who'd subsequently left the firm and a client who was so obscure they sounded like a small local doughnut company. Practice areas often had no content and it was sometimes hard to see if the firm had any expertise in its listed areas of activity. Worse still, how to contact the firm, who to contact and their phone number was hard to find. And when, eventually, it was possible to find an email address, it was a generic info@) address. That might have been ok as it promised next day response but the info@ inbox was rarely checked so genuine enquiries from prospective new clients most usually went unanswered!

And while the new staff/careers section was a bit more dynamic and up to date, it had little information and the key social web sites for aspiring lawyers like RollonFriday and LawCareers carried content from most of the rival firms but nothing from this one.

The list of site negatives went on and on and it was only when the senior partner group saw the hard evidence that they did finally agree, and still somewhat reluctantly, to invest in a site update and revitalised online presence. And here is a firm with a turnover of more than £1bn and individual partner profit at around £400k per partner (and no debt and very cash flow positive) hesitating about spending around £500k on an investment which their prospective clients are saying is the item that most influences their initial selection.

What they had not realised was just how quickly online information and presentation had become engrained and entrenched and how business habits had changed so fast that the proverbial "tipping point" had been reached. Old fashioned networks and traditional contacts had not been displaced. But they had been added to. And in a material way. Client selection was now "multi-channel" and certainly contained an important digital information component. This had become so vital but the lawyers, immersed in their day-to-day arcane world, had not realised it. They needed the wake-up call!

But this situation is not that untypical. There remains the view that the real B2B activity is still done via a sales force with face to face contact and people who build long term relationships. And nothing wrong with that. But most customers, as the law firm found out, are starting to expect more and more online information. And they expect that to be smartly presented. It's "the face of the firm" to the outside world. They expect extranet facilities where they can check on progress of any joint activities. They expect My Account features so they can look at purchase history, invoice status, payment and receipts. They expect special news updates which are relevant to them and their business. They want content and site material configured for use on their iPad and iPhone, they demand an excellent search facility that lets them find exactly what they want quickly and easily. If Company X is not offering these sort of tools and functions then for sure there's a Company Y knocking on the door with just these sort of initiatives.

●**Case Study 8: other B2B examples:**

HP: a good site with lots of information and links. But a contact phone number that only works Monday to Friday 9 till 5. It's another example of an old-fashioned approach. In the "good old days", customers had no expectation of being able to do business outside of weekdays 9 till 5. But today's world is all about the "convenience of now". We want to be able to contact, discover, network, organise meetings and network at a time that suits us. We maybe overseas, we may be discussing business partners with our colleagues and deciding who to shortlist or call. We expect 24/7 access and response.

Cisco.com: a very good example of a strong B2B focussed web site. There is clear product and service information on the site, a multi-channel contact strategy with call centre and partner locator by region, support documentation and video guides, listing of training, events and professional certification, webcasts and seminars, a "My Cisco" account centre for customers which is the privileged access and content area, plus a How to Buy call to action. It works. It's their fifth generation web site and continues to evolve and improve. It sits alongside a broad and strong web presence which includes a solid search engine first page presence and clear viral social networking policy. Cisco can be followed on YouTube at YouTube.com/CiscoPR, they have their own blogs at http://blogs.cisco.com, there is the Cisco Networking academy on Facebook as well as separate Cisco Retail and Cisco Systems Facebook pages proudly proclaiming it's now reached over 100,000 "likes", there is a Cisco "superfan" programme to promote positive influencers and networkers, there's a "tourguide" on an official Twitter feed and there are additional Twitter-based initiatives on CiscoLiveEurope and CiscoSystems.

Every company needs its seminal moment or wake up call. For Cisco it came some years ago. They did their annual sales analysis, looking at who had been their biggest customers and they suddenly realised that one of them, who had done some $100m of business with them that year, had in fact never received a sales call or sales rep visit. Immediately the traditional reactions kicked-in: this is a big customer, let's arrange a high level meeting, we can talk long term strategy and extended product sales. But when they called to set things up they were told: love the products, love the support but we like to do business online and we'd like to stick with that. Just keep updating the web site!

There have for some years now been a very developed set of global trading web sites which manage a growing share of world trade in exports and imports. Alibaba.com regularly wins awards for best global B2B site as it seeks to match buyers and sellers across a wide range of products from Chemicals, Agriculture equipment, Commodities and ingredients to Olive oil, apples and all the way through to fashion accessories. It's the world's best bazaar! Other sites have more specialist regional or product focus eg TradeIndia and TradeEgypt or ResearchChemicalsShop.

All this simply recognises that the web does play an extraordinary part in B2B commerce whether it's directly selling or influencing the sale or extending a Brand's reach and business development potential. Now B2B is getting much more attention. Google was voted "best B2B brand", beating out Apple.com/Business, Office Depot/ Viking Direct, Experian.com and AccountancyAge.com. Each of these had recently rebuilt and established clear actionable B2B web sites with extended web presence through a selected mix of campaigns, search marketing excellence, social media activity and connected multi-channel contact programmes.

A recent "brand health check" carried out by Havas showed that those companies with demonstrated excellence online, the vanguard companies, are still, despite all the case studies, a minority! In their research, spanning over 30,000 people across 4 continents, they found that only 30% of today's largest Brands were considered to have "a meaningful and relevant online presence". And when asked to consider the consequences of that most of the respondents said that if the brand had no engagement online then they would just go to a rival brand or company that did!

Many Brands are still not living up to expectations or to standards set by leading organisations: "digital, indirect and social communications including peer comment are now becoming pivotal platforms to fuel the necessary brand dialogue with customers and engage and build trust… there's a real opportunity for companies to shift from "relying on traditional marketing" to start building relevant brand engagement initiatives that can capture more of the collective will and be proactive to encourage existing and prospective customer interaction"

These "Brand Health" checks by the likes of Havas are becoming ever more popular and here's a basic checklist to assess a Brand's modern relevance and sustainability:

1. Find out where your customers are connecting with your Brand. That's the kind of brand audit and "buzz monitoring" discussed previously.

2. Understand how customers are using the Web. What are they looking for when they search? Is it product details, do they want to browse and research or are they looking to buy, is it after sales service, maintenance contracts, complaints or returns, contact details etc? All this can be discovered through basic web analysis packages that monitor page views and visits, dwell times and drop-off points. And it can be supplemented with basic customer research, whether a one-off evening focus group, a quick online survey (eg SurveyMonkey.com) or more detailed Havas type global research

3. What is today's perception of the Brand? Again the buzz monitoring and sentiment indices alongside any supplemental research can immediately identify strengths and weaknesses

4. What are key competitors up to? If you take most B2C products and services there is a huge amount of investment, improvement and learning taking place and there is just no room for inaction, underinvestment or complacency. The B2B world has also experienced waves of innovation, though as our law firm found, it's been possible to get away with doing nothing, until now!

5. Recognise the social media shift and that customers now do have more control over the brand's future. A strong, vigorous, proactive and adequately funded and resourced social media strategy and plan is critical for this coming decade. Just setting up a page on Facebook is not the answer! There's a growing body of case study evidence to show just how much positive impact a strategic and invested social media plan can have.

★ ★ ★ ★

The internet future and the digital technology world is an exciting one. It's already well-established and the fact that it contributes so much today to GDP and has so much economic potential in the future shows just how pervasive and unstoppable is its reach and momentum. Many companies are under pressure to manage budgets and investment conservatively, but it will be hard to resist the lure of digital technology innovation as that is driving all the growth and will be the core source of competitive advantage into the future.